A Cry
From the Heart

The Bahá'ís in Iran

by

WILLIAM SEARS

GEORGE RONALD
OXFORD

GEORGE RONALD, Publisher
46 High Street, Kidlington, Oxford, OX5 2DN

ISBN 0-85398-133-7 (cloth)
ISBN 0-85398-134-5 (paper)

Printed in Great Britain by Richard Clay
(The Chaucer Press) Ltd,
Bungay, Suffolk

942729

Contents

Introduction

The persecution of the Bahá'í community in Iran has recently become so savage as to attract the attention of governments, international councils, the media and the United Nations. The present outburst is conducted in an organized way with the evident purpose of exterminating an entire community, the largest religious minority in the country; indeed, larger than the Jewish, Zoroastrian and Christian communities together. The leaders of the Bahá'í community have been seized and executed, its holy places razed, its properties and financial assets attached, many homes burned, the crops of its farmers destroyed, its members denied employment and its children expelled from schools.

A Cry from the Heart is an impassioned account of the horrors perpetrated against an innocent people. It is written by an eminent Western Bahá'í who has travelled extensively in Iran visiting the Bahá'í community there. It is a refutation of the false and contradictory charges levelled against them, and an exposé of the genocidal purpose of the present outbreak. It is up to date and authentic.

1

Núk

Muḥammad-Ḥusayn and <u>Sh</u>ikkar-Nisá' had just returned to their house after a long, hard day's work in the fields of their farm. Their name is Ma'ṣúmí. They lived in a tiny little almost forgotten hamlet, a spot on the road, called Núk.

Remember it. It rhymes with '*wonderful*'!

The story begins on November 22, 1980. Seven months before I began writing these pages.

A full moon was shining and splashing its friendly light on the few scattered houses of their small village. Muḥammad and <u>Sh</u>ikkar-Nisá' washed away the stains of their day's work, said their prayers and ate their dinner. They had left-over mutton from a sheep which had been smoked the previous day to be used during the cold, bitter winter when times would be hard.

After dinner they shelled almonds with a small hammer, preparing a store for the winter. It was a cheerful noise. They laughed and talked as they worked.

It was well after nine o'clock when they had just decided to take their tea.

<u>Sh</u>ikkar-Nisá' prepared the samovar, lighted the fire under it, and they resumed their shelling, waiting for the water to boil. They had done it a thousand times. It was one of the most pleasant and peaceful times of the day. Relaxing, recuperating, resting the aching bones after a day's work well done. It was a time to be grateful.

At that happy moment between husband and wife, their lives were almost at an end.

Masked and armed men were scaling the garden wall. They moved silently and stealthily toward the house.

The sound of the hammer on the almond shells as Muḥammad and Shikkar-Nisá' laughed and competed with each other drowned out the careful approach of the killers.

It was like a scene from Shakespeare:

Enter First Murderer!

It was 10.00 p.m. exactly. November 22, 1980.

The moon was in full splendour when Muḥammad-Ḥusayn said, 'I must go to the stable and fill the feeding trough for the sheep.'

'Hurry back,' Shikkar-Nisá' told him, 'or your tea will be cold.'

It was the last time she would see her husband alive, the last words she would ever say to him.

Shikkar-Nisá' swept up the almonds, and started to finish her own tea, when she heard the outside door open. There was a curtain across the inner door, so she called out:

'Muḥammad?'

No reply.

Suddenly, several masked men swept into the room.

In the dim light of the kerosene lamp, Shikkar-Nisá' could not tell they were masked. She turned to them with a smile. She liked people. Even unexpected visitors.

As they moved into the light, Shikkar-Nisá' saw they were masked. She cried out, dropped her half-filled glass of tea to the floor, and tried to escape. They seized her roughly by the arms and dragged her across the room. She cried out.

'Muḥammad!'

One of the masked men choked her to keep her quiet.

Shikkar-Nisá' moaned. She begged them not to hurt her husband. Do whatever they wanted to her, she cried, but don't harm Muḥammad. Her pleas went unanswered. They choked off further comment.

Still no word had yet been spoken by the attackers. Masks can cover the face; spoken words can identify the speakers.

The marauders carried a heavy wooden door from the corner of the house. They tied Shikkar-Nisá' tightly with rope, placed the door on top of her, placed dry wood on top of the door, poured the contents of a kerosene lamp over the wood, and splashed her clothing.

Even when she realized that they intended to burn her alive, her only thought was for the safety of her husband, Muḥammad.

The arsonists threw a lighted match. The fumes flashed into fire. They watched until they were sure the flames were high enough to burn Shikkar-Nisá' to ashes in a short time. With a grunt of satisfaction, they left. It was only part of their night's work.

Now, it was Muḥammad's turn.

They knew exactly where to find him.

Shikkar-Nisá' tried to scream and warn him. It was useless.

She later told her neighbours, 'My whole life, a flood of memories, the children growing up, all passed through my mind. Strangely enough, my fear turned to calm, as I waited for the flames. I could think only of my husband, Muḥammad. I cried out in anguish and prayer.'

Shikkar-Nisá' knew they were being killed because they were Bahá'ís. They had been warned that it was dangerous to be a Bahá'í these days. What days was it not, in Iran? It would be wiser, they were told, to give up their Faith. They always gently but firmly refused. They were now paying for it.

The heat surrounding Shikkar-Nisá' became intense. The pain almost unendurable. But the flames reached the nylon ropes, melted them, and S̲h̲ikkar-Nisá' was able to free herself.

Half of her body was burned and charred. Crying and moaning, she seized her husband's overcoat, wrapped herself in it, and ran outside. She couldn't find Muḥammad anywhere. She rushed to the nearest house for help.

The neighbours cautiously opened the door. They were not Bahá'ís and it was dangerous to become involved in things that happened at night. They were horrified to see her terrible condition, and their children started crying.

S̲h̲ikkar-Nisá' told them what had happened. She asked them please to help her find her husband. They refused to leave the house. They were afraid. One man, however, did agree to go up on the roof to see what he could.

He could see nothing, he said, even though the moon was full.

S̲h̲ikkar-Nisá' realized they did not intend to help her. She borrowed a hurricane lamp and, carrying it in her burned hands, rushed out to begin her own search. Along the road, she saw a crumpled form fallen in a ditch. It was her dear husband, Muḥammad.

'I found to my horror,' S̲h̲ikkar-Nisá' later wept, 'that I was too late! He was dead. He had been burned to death in the path of his Beloved.'

Neighbours said later that many of them had heard Muḥammad-Ḥusayn's cries of anguish as the masked murderers had seized him and set him afire. The neighbours had gone to their windows and opened their doors to peep out to see what was happening. They admitted witnessing the death of this brave man, but no one had gone to his rescue. He and his wife were Bahá'ís, after all, and Bahá'ís were in trouble with the authorities. They were probably spies, as people said, and deserved to die.

When S̲h̲ikkar-Nisá' saw the charred body of her dear husband, she wept bitterly.

'This is a heartless, cruel murder,' she said to those few who had finally come out of their houses to see what had happened. 'We have shown you nothing but love and kindness for all these years, and you have done this terrible thing to us.'

She knew it had not been strangers hiding behind those masks.

Silently, everyone returned to his home. Not one neighbour would stay to help poor Shikkar-Nisá' take the body of her murdered husband home. No one even volunteered to inform her son-in-law who lived in Zirk, a neighbouring village, half a mile away.

Witnesses reported that the ringleader was startled and alarmed to see Shikkar-Nisá' still alive and standing by the ditch. He was afraid she might be able to identify him. Seeing her alone, after the neighbours had left, he hurried to her side as though to help. Shikkar-Nisá' was weeping.

They reported later that this criminal tried to finish off the helpless woman by striking her violently before rushing off. After he left, Shikkar-Nisá' could no longer talk. She had lost the power of speech.

In the middle of the night this poor, half-burned woman, broken-hearted, hardly able to walk, was forced to abandon the charred remains of her husband. No one would help. Slowly she made her way home, and locked herself alone in the now empty house.

Her son-in-law came the next day.

He found his father-in-law lying in the ditch covered with ashes, his face black with soot. He was told more of the tragic story by eyewitnesses who were not as afraid to talk in the daylight as they had been in the dark.

The murderers, they said, had soaked Muḥammad-Ḥusayn with fuel, and set him ablaze. Then they began shouting at him:

'Run! Run!'

The piteous man, already a human torch, ran as best he could. He fell into the ditch, crying with the agony of

Sh̲ikkar-Nisá'

Muḥammad-Ḥusayn

pain. They piled wood on top of him, splashed it with more kerosene, and burned him to death. Delighted with their night's work, they warmed themselves by the fire before leaving.

S̲h̲ikkar-Nisá' still could not speak. Her only response to her son-in-law's first questions was the tears which flowed down her cheeks as she kept pointing toward the place where Muḥammad had been murdered. She was so terribly burned that she had to be carefully wrapped in a blanket and taken in that fashion on the bus to the hospital.

By then she was in a coma, and she died six days later.

S̲h̲ikkar-Nisá' is buried with her martyred husband, Muḥammad-Ḥusayn, side by side, united in death as they were in life.

Look at them Núk, these two darling souls. They are from your village.

Such a tiny little place, who would ever know what you did there? It seemed safe to kill them, didn't it? Who would ever find out?

Now, you know. The whole world has found out. Your brave victory is being shared with people in more than a hundred thousand places in the world, and with their friends in a hundred thousand more. Everywhere knows about Núk today. Everybody. Everywhere. Even the name of the ringleader of the arsonists and murderers is known. His mask has been removed.

No, he won't be punished for his crime. Not in Iran. After all, those they killed were only Bahá'ís; the only two Bahá'ís in the village.

2

A Cry from the Heart

The Bahá'ís in Iran are my personal friends. I have met many of them face to face, stayed in their homes, played with their children, attended their meetings, marvelled at their heroic history and felt the warmth of their love and kindness. They are at this very moment the victims of a ruthless campaign of persecution and terrorism designed to exterminate them in the land of their birth.

That is why I am writing this book.

There is nothing official about it. It is strictly personal. It is exactly what the title says it is: a cry from the heart!

What you will like most about it is that I don't want anything. I'm not asking for your money, your time, or your support. I don't want you to intervene on behalf of my fellow Bahá'ís in Iran. I am not asking you for a single thing.

You may find that refreshing!

As the author, I will not receive any royalties or money from it.

Of course I do want you to read the book, and if it meets with your interest, to share it with your friends.

You know what is happening to *my* friends.

That is why I call my book *A Cry from the Heart*.

Recent events in Iran (the ancient land of Persia) have focussed the attention of the world's mass media on it. The Bahá'í Faith has been mentioned frequently, prominently, and always inaccurately by spokesmen of the present regime in Iran.

I am referring to the official spokesmen and to their interviews in North America, South America, and Europe. They have made many misleading statements and false accusations against the Bahá'í Faith in the press, and on both radio and television.

These false statements have been made not unwittingly, unintentionally, or mistakenly. By no means. They were not innocent or accidental. They were deliberate. They are all part of a carefully conceived, well-organized, nation-wide plan of extermination, the purpose of which is to wipe out an entire religious minority, namely, the Bahá'í community in Iran, and to do it without letting the world become aware that this is their purpose, one to which they are wholly committed and dedicated.

As a former television and radio performer, I know the tremendous influence and impact of the media. I shudder to think what a dreadfully false picture of the Bahá'í Faith is being created in the minds of those who see, hear or read these damaging reports.

Even the members of my own family, and friends who were not Bahá'ís, have become upset and concerned. They recognized the misrepresentations, of course, but were annoyed that no one was crying, 'Foul!'

I was furious myself.

I said: 'Enough is enough!'

And that is how I came to write *A Cry from the Heart*. It was the start of my campaign: one Bahá'í against injustice.

Personal. Individual. Unofficial.

I decided not to let these deliberate misrepresentations, made so craftily and persistently against such a sweet, soul-stirring, world-healing Faith which I love, go unanswered any longer. I decided to tell the man on the street and the great masses of mankind exactly what was happening in Iran, and *why*.

The Founders of the Bahá'í Faith, its early teachers, its heroes and heroines, its martyrs and saints were all, of course, Persian. Consequently no country in all the world is dearer to Bahá'ís than Iran. But when writing of the outrages visited on my co-religionists there I may get a little salty on my own, and express a few sincere personal feelings about these outrages. This will not, however, change the fundamental, universal principles of love and unity which are part of every Bahá'í life, and every Bahá'í community in the world, including Iran.

I do not plan to be detached or serenely objective. I am going to turn over the flat rock, so be prepared.

The atrocities taking place against Bahá'ís today throughout Iran are no longer matters of suspicion or opinion. They are matters of fact. The proof can be found in the records of libraries, newsrooms, United Nations Agencies, human rights organizations, telex and cable files in every part of the world.

The spotlight of world publicity has now been turned directly upon Iran. It is no longer a secret that the killings, burnings, lootings, and torture of Bahá'ís are still continuing, even as these pages are being written. It is no longer possible for the persecutors to suppress or minimize the enormity of their crimes, or to hide anonymously behind the fiction of 'uncontrollable mobs'.

Those days are over!

Confiscation of property, of bank accounts, burning and looting of homes, officially sanctioned executions of innocent victims – all these things take place everywhere, in the streets, in the market-place, and in the homes.

The Bahá'ís are harassed, beaten, abused, killed. Sometimes husband and wife together. Or an entire family. Or a group of close friends, or neighbours, or business associates. Chosen at random. At the whim of the killers.

Stabbed, stoned, hanged, burned alive, hacked to pieces with knives, stood before firing-squads.

Men, women, children. No one is spared.

Their crime?

They are Bahá'ís.

These attacks have been going on for nearly one hundred and fifty years.

The first onslaught of the current persecutions began in 1978. It is now in its fourth year. The severity and spread of the outrages increase each day and become ever more sinister. There is no end in sight, and no sign of a let-up.

What is most alarming and threatening about the present avalanche is not its violence; that has always occurred. It is the devilish ingenuity of the assault designed to eliminate an entire community of nearly half a million souls. The terror has now spread into every level of Bahá'í life, to city dweller, villager and farmer.

At first the Bahá'í business houses, the repository of the savings of rich and poor Bahá'ís alike, were confiscated, with no recompense. Then the great Bahá'í hospital in Teheran, built, operated and fully supported by Bahá'ís, where patients of all religions and backgrounds were treated with the same loving care, was taken over. Next, Bahá'í holy places throughout the country were occupied and put to whatever use, often personal, the revolutionary authorities, equally often the man with a gun, might decide. The meeting-places of the local communities were next to be taken. Then, having deprived this helpless community, which has no rights in law, of its funds, hospital, holy places and religious properties, attention was turned to the leaders of the community. All nine members of the National Spiritual Assembly were kidnapped (see p. 211) and have not been heard of, except by rumour, to this day. Outstanding Bahá'ís in the provincial communities were next and many of those have been executed. The obvious aim is to get rid of the capable, trusted, elected leaders before launching the attack on the rank and file.

The Bahá'í community they are trying to destroy is the

largest religious minority in Iran. It has more members than the Christian, Jewish and Zoroastrian communities combined. In spite of this, the Bahá'í Faith is not recognized and Bahá'ís are deprived of their basic human rights. There is no one and no place in the entire country they can approach for protection. They cannot appeal to the clergy, to the courts, or to the authorities. The clergy and their religious courts *are* the authorities.

They are engaged in a process which the entire civilized world has always been against.

It is called: *Genocide!*

In the first half of this century, a society was founded in Iran for the purpose of exterminating the Bahá'ís in that country. Its members were motivated solely by religious fanaticism and hatred. They called themselves the Society for the Promotion of Islam but have been publicly referred to by a leading ayatollah, Shaykh Ali Teherani, as the anti-Bahá'í Society. For a number of years they were a loosely-knit force, taking any convenient opportunity to harass and kill Bahá'ís. In the 1940s however, they began to suspect the advantages of organization and from then on became not only the sworn enemies of the Bahá'í Faith but the constant prodders of the authorities to move against its unprotected members. They instigated the pogrom of 1955 and are behind the present scheme of extermination. The authorities, complaisant before and always ready to use the Bahá'ís as scapegoats to divert attention from the general condition of life in Iran, are now, in the new regime of die-hard ayatollahs, more than willing to give full reign to these fanatics.

Authorized and approved terrorists are brutalizing and victimizing members of the Bahá'í Faith in villages and towns across the face of the entire country. Hundreds, their properties looted, burned or confiscated, are fleeing from rural areas to seek refuge in the larger cities.

Even as these pages are being written.

Death has been brought to Bahá'ís by the use of

Guns
Axes
Knives
Stoning
Stabbing
Strangling
Beating to death with fists, boots and clubs
Hanging
Hacking to death with spades and shovels
Burning alive (both men and women)
Firing-squads

The knowledge of this annihilation plot has already gone round the world. The catalogue of Persian persecutions is well known everywhere. They are being watched, hour by hour, day by day.

What the fanatics do not seem to have realized is the great world-wide spread of the Bahá'í Faith. They are so blinded by their passionate hatred for the Bahá'í community in Iran, and their determination to uproot it, that they seem almost totally unaware of the phenomenal growth it has achieved in the world. Very likely they would be astonished to know that the things which they hate and detest the most about the Bahá'ís are the very things for which the Bahá'í Faith is admired and respected in the world outside Iran.

There are Bahá'í communities, some tiny, some very big, in more than one hundred thousand centres in almost every part of the planet, all raising their cries of indignation and protest.

The Bahá'í International Community at the United Nations, where the Bahá'ís enjoy 'consultative status' among the Non-Governmental Organizations of ECOSOC, is taking the lead in calling the attention of the world's nations, governments and leaders of thought to the persecution of the Bahá'í community now taking place in Iran. A number of sovereign governments, as well as associations such as the European Economic Community and the European Parliament, human rights organizations and humanitarian societies have made representations to the authorities in Iran.

Many others have arisen spontaneously to add their voices of protest, not because they were especially for the Bahá'ís, but because they were against all forms of persecution and oppression.

To them all, without exception, I offer my warmest appreciation on behalf of my beleaguered brothers and sisters.

The Bahá'í World Community has already expressed its official thanks.

We are grateful.

This book, however, has quite a different purpose.

It is not an appeal to those in positions of influence, power or authority. It is not a formal, reasoned White Paper to be shared with the leaders of men, or an elegant diplomatic response to the horrendous happenings that are taking the lives of my fellow Bahá'ís in Iran.

Far from it.

It is a call to the people of the world, the masses of mankind, to the final court of human appeal.

I have great confidence in the man on the street. I want him to know the truth. In the future, whenever the name Iran is mentioned, and the name Bahá'í is associated with it, I want every man, woman and child in the entire world to be able to tell the '*good guys*' from the '*bad guys*'.

You are about to find out which is which.

You make the decision.

3

Attacks and Accusations

You will be thinking, 'What is this all about?' 'Who are these Bahá'ís and what do they believe to arouse such passions?' The answer is plain and simple. Bahá'ís believe that a new messenger from God has come to bring about the long-promised unity and brotherhood of all mankind – the Kingdom promised by Christ and confirmed by Muhammad. And that is anathema to the Muslim clergy in Iran. Their response is fanatical hatred: kill, torture, exterminate.

One of their worst attempts was made in 1955 when the Shah's regime was only halted by the personal intervention of the Secretary-General of the United Nations, Mr Dag Hammarskjöld. In the face of world opinion the Shah restrained the mullas. Now they have overthrown him and are not worried by world opinion, and they pursue their avowed intention to erase forever the Bahá'í community in Iran, and to extinguish permanently its light.

Of course you don't believe what I'm saying. Not yet. But before this book is ended, I think you *will* believe it.

This scheme is quite simple. Extermination.

The list of each and every one of their violations of religious freedom and human rights guaranteed by the documents which their country subscribed to at the United Nations is known the world over. A detailed record of all abuses is being kept.

Among the current persecutions of the Bahá'í commu-

17

nity in Iran – oppressions already recorded and protested to Iranian embassies, chargés d'affaires and foreign ministers of governments – are the following:

1. Illegal arrests without warrants
2. Wholesale imprisonments
    without proper charges and authority;
    of Bahá'í lawyers who come to defend those arrested;
    with prisoners held incommunicado, their whereabouts unknown to families and friends
3. Illegal trials with no chance for proper defence
4. Illegal, summary executions
5. Last Wills and Testaments, hastily written by those to die, withheld from survivors and families
6. Houses broken into by masked marauders who threaten, beat, and sometimes kill
7. Homes confiscated, looted, contents auctioned off and proceeds kept by authorities or looters
8. Houses, several score across the land, burned to the ground; families evicted, left homeless, their children included
9. Private possessions of victims seized and sold; even personal jewellery stripped away and either kept or sold
10. Kidnappings of well-known and loved Bahá'ís, their whereabouts unknown
11. Businesses invaded, closed, sold, sometimes burned; monies kept
12. Private bank accounts confiscated
13. Children ridiculed in the streets, insulted, beaten, expelled from schools, denied education, and made homeless in many parts of the land
14. Bahá'í marriages not recognized
15. Bahá'í farms destroyed; farmers chased off their land

16. Orchards levelled to the ground*
17. Crops burned*
18. Cattle and livestock slaughtered
19. Radio and television describe the 'punishment' of Bahá'ís as treatment given to criminals

These attacks are not diminishing. The increase in number is gravely alarming, both in their intensity and spread.

The entire Bahá'í community in Iran is under fierce fire, and is fighting for its very life. As I write this the following message has been sent from the Bahá'í World Centre to the Bahá'ís all over the world:

PERSECUTION BAHA'IS IRAN GAINING MOMENTUM ENTERING NEW PHASE: IN YAZD A FEW DAYS AGO GOVERNMENT FROZE ALL ASSETS 117 BELIEVERS. ON 8 AUGUST ANNOUNCEMENT ON LOCAL RADIO SUMMONED HEADS 150 PROMINENT BAHA'I FAMILIES TO REPORT WITHIN ONE WEEK TO REVOLUTIONARY AUTHORITIES. IN ABSENTIA DECREES TO BE ISSUED RESPECT ANY NAMED BELIEVER WHO FAILS PRESENT HIMSELF BY 15 AUGUST. AMONG NAMES ARE FEW WHO PASSED AWAY, CONFIRMING DETERMINATION AUTHORITIES PERSECUTE BAHA'IS PURELY FOR THEIR BELIEF, NOT BECAUSE OF ANY ALLEGED CRIME. ONE OF THOSE NAMED WAS ARRESTED AS HE WAS PROCEEDING FOR NECESSARY TEMPORARY JOURNEY OUTSIDE YAZD. ACTIONS TAKEN FORESHADOW PLAN AUTHORITIES FORCE BAHA'IS RECANT THEIR FAITH ON PAIN CONFISCATION ALL THEIR PROPERTIES, OTHER DIRE CONSEQUENCES. URGE SHARE NEWS THESE OMINOUS DEVELOPMENTS WITH YOUR GOVERNMENT GIVE WIDE COVERAGE NEWS MEDIA HELP CON-

---

* They ignore the guidance of their own Holy Book: '... *but agress not: God loves not the aggressors.*' (Koran 2: line 187, A. J. Arberry, *The Koran Interpreted,* London, 1955). A footnote to this Sura in another translation explains: 'In any case strict limits must not be transgressed ... nor trees and crops cut down.' These are the people who accuse the Bahá'ís of being against Islam, the Koran, and Muhammad.

VINCE AUTHORITIES STAY HAND OPPRESSION DIRECTED MEMBERS INNOCENT COMMUNITY.

FURTHER REPORT JUST RECEIVED INDICATES IN MANSHAD VILLAGE NEAR YAZD GOVERNMENT OFFICIAL FROM YAZD ACCOMPANIED REVOLUTIONARY GUARDS HAS PEREMPTORILY SEIZED FURNITURE CROPS LIVESTOCK LOCAL BELIEVERS.

FOLLOWING DETAILS ADDITIONAL PERSECUTIONS OTHER PROVINCES NOW IN HAND:
  IN MASJID SULAYMAN AUTHORITIES HAVE INSTRUCTED BANKS SUBMIT LIST ALL CHECKING AND DEPOSIT ACCOUNTS BAHA'IS.
  IN NAYSHABUR WHERE TWO BELIEVERS WERE RECENTLY MARTYRED MOB HAD DESTROYED WALL BAHA'I CEMETERY. AUTHORITIES NOW CLAIM TWO MILLION RIALS FROM LOCAL COMMUNITY TO RESTORE WALL.
  IN HIMMAT-ABAD NEAR ABADIH WIVES OF BELIEVERS WHO HAD FLED FROM THEIR HOMES HAVE BEEN GIVEN NOTICE CALL THEIR HUSBANDS. WIVES THREATENED GRAVE REPERCUSSIONS IF HUSBANDS FAIL PRESENT THEMSELVES.
ADD ABOVE ADDITIONAL ITEMS TO APPEAL YOUR GOVERNMENT AND MEDIA BUT MAIN EMPHASIS SHOULD BE PERILOUS SITUATION YAZD, UNKNOWN FATE SOME SEVEN SCORE DEVOTED BELIEVERS. HOPEFUL IMMEDIATE ACTION WILL FORESTALL DANGEROUS CONSEQUENCES BEFORE SATURDAY 15 AUGUST.

I know that a great many other people in Iran are being killed because they are displeasing to the revolutionary regime, but there is one very important difference between them and the Bahá'ís. *They* have no choice but to face the firing-squad. The Bahá'ís have. If they will renounce their Faith and say they are Muslims, or even just not Bahá'ís, they can go free.

Their homes and looted possessions will be restored to them: those that have not been burned or sold. Their businesses will be restored to them: those that have not been dismantled or burned. Their bank accounts will be given back: those that have not already been spent or shared among the arsonists, looters, and official confiscators.

The villagers, farmers and needy Bahá'ís who invested their tiny incomes in these Bahá'í companies to protect their future with pensions will, of course, be taken care of.

'Taken care of', to a Bahá'í in Iran, can mean almost anything.

If individual Bahá'ís will recant and deny their Faith they are promised a much brighter future. Their children will be able to return to school: those who are well enough, and who haven't been expelled permanently.

The firing-squads will be called off. The violence will cease. The 'uncontrollable' mobs will be controlled. No further killings of Bahá'ís will either be authorized or permitted.

All the Bahá'í is required to say is that one simple phrase:

'I am not a Bahá'í.'

No more nonsense about spying for Israel, or having supported Savak, or the Shah's regime; we all know those things were just part of the game. The real issue is that you are a Bahá'í. Just say you are not and you'll be free, and you will be exonerated from the charges against you.

As an added incentive to encourage this nation-wide denial of faith, the Bahá'ís in Iran have now been given yet another ultimatum:

'Either renounce your Faith, and say that you are not Bahá'ís, or surrender the deeds to all your properties. If you refuse, they will be taken from you by force. Your houses will either be sold or burned.'

The Bahá'ís must either recant and thus put an end to their Faith in Iran, or surrender all they own, home, property, and possessions, so there will be no roots for them to put down for their families, and thus the Bahá'í Faith will perish.

The authorities in Iran leave the Bahá'ís no other choice. It is one or the other, with a death here and there to encourage the stubborn.

To assist further the truly obstinate Bahá'ís in making their renunciations, masked enforcers who specialize in brutality and spirit-breaking, force their way into Bahá'í homes in the dead of night. They appear masked and armed. Suddenly they are standing over the bed, awakening father, mother and children.

They arouse the entire family to the sound of loud voices and the display of guns, threatening their lives while they are still dazed with sleep.

The terrorists warn the family that everyone is about to be killed. This includes the children who, still rubbing their sleepy eyes, have no idea what it is all about. Only that it's hard to be a Bahá'í.

The masked marauders raise their weapons and fire. It is the noise of thunder. Terrifying. The children cry. You wonder why you are not dead.

Then you realize that they have missed you deliberately. This time.

Laughing all the while, enjoying the murder-game, they fire at you, your wife and the children a second time. Again they miss. More laughter. Next time, they warn, it will mean death. The end of your entire family. Unless you recant.

'We will be back,' they threaten.

They tell you exactly what will happen then to you and your entire family unless you all either deny your Faith, or surrender the titles and deeds to all your property and resources.

The fun is over. The masked torturers leave. More threats at the door. Another volley. Another miss. More raucous laughter as they disappear into the night, leaving the children shaking and terrified.

It is time for you to pray. And for your children to cry. They *will* come again.

They do.
This time they kill.

I have listed below the major accusations made currently against the Bahá'í Faith in Iran.

I plan to answer clearly, categorically, and completely, every one of these baseless and false accusations. I shall deal with them one at a time, and shall, I believe, by showing how fraudulent they are, demolish their absurd and grotesque misrepresentations of the Bahá'í Faith.

I mean business, and do not plan to avoid any of these false charges, however absurd and shameful.

I have not listed them in any particular order. I have merely emphasized those which have been repeated most often and most insultingly during the present attacks.

Accusations

1. The Bahá'í Faith, far from being a religion, is a subversive and heretical sect which plans to establish its own regime in Iran.
2. The Bahá'í Faith is a political party which supported the regime of Muhammad Reza Shah, and received favours from him.
3. The Bahá'ís are agents of foreign powers, such as the United States and Russia, and of British imperialism.
4. The Bahá'ís are 'spies' for Israel, and secretly collaborate with international Zionism. They contribute financially to the support of Israel which aids that country against its Arab and Muslim neighbours.
5. The Bahá'ís have their World Centre in Israel, and therefore must be hostile to Iran and to the current Islamic Revolution.
6. The Bahá'ís travel frequently to and from Israel, carrying and receiving information against Iran and other Arab nations.

7. The Bahá'ís are against Islam and Muhammad, the Prophet of Islam, and insult His holy Book, the Koran.

8. There have been Bahá'ís in high places in the political life of Iran, although they claim they do not become involved in politics. A Bahá'í was once Prime Minister. Others served in lesser ministerial capacities.

9. The Bahá'ís of Iran are quite different from those in other lands. In Iran they are politically oriented.

10. One of the heads of the dreaded secret police, Savak, and others of its high-ranking officers, have been members of the Bahá'í Faith.

11. Et cetera, et cetera, et cetera.

Those ten will do for a start. Lesser false charges, we are sure, will be washed out to sea as a fringe benefit of finding the basic ten accusations totally erroneous and completely false.

Some of my public-relations friends have told me, 'It's a mistake to list all ten of those charges against your Faith. Even if they're not true.'

'Why?'

'Because many people probably don't *know* about all of them.'

'Good! I want them to know. And the sooner I get at the refutations the better.'

4

Refutation

ACCUSATION

The Bahá'í Faith is a subversive and heretical sect. It wishes to set up its own regime in Iran, and overthrow the present government. Therefore no punishment is too severe for such an enemy of Iran.

THE TRUTH

If the authorities in Iran had read the papers, documents and books which they have confiscated from so many Bahá'í Centres, instead of destroying them, as well as burning and vandalizing the Bahá'í properties which they have entered unlawfully, they would have known that fundamental Bahá'í teaching which forbids its followers to take part in any subversive activity or to be members of political parties.

Forbids, not discourages.

Loyalty to government under all circumstances, even beneath the dreadful scourge of the persecutions visited upon them by the present authorities in Iran, does not change this belief. Loyalty to government is absolutely basic and binding upon every Bahá'í. It is one of the most fundamental Bahá'í principles.

The Bahá'í teachings, which are the same for every country in the world, state plainly and emphatically that

> In every country where any of this people reside, they must behave towards the government of that country

25

with loyalty, honesty and truthfulness. This is that which hath been revealed at the behest of Him Who is the Ordainer, the Ancient of Days.

The contention that the Bahá'í Faith is not a religion, but a heretical sect, has been used by the Iranian authorities ever since its birth, to justify their inhuman treatment of its members. The question is best answered by those who are not Bahá'ís, but who are specialists in the field of religion and history.

The world-famous historian, Arnold Toynbee, has written about the Bahá'í Faith as a religion, saying:

> My opinion is that (1) Bahá'ism is undoubtedly a religion. (2) Bahá'ism is an independent religion, on a par with Islám, Christianity, and the other recognized world religions. Bahá'ism is not a sect of some other religion; it is a separate religion, and has the same status as other recognized religions.

Except in Iran, that is.

The successive regimes in Iran have done all in their power to convince themselves and the world that the Bahá'í Faith is a 'sect' and not an independent world religion. To get people to believe it has become more and more difficult for them.

It is much easier to deprive an obscure sect of all its human rights, than an independent religion on a par with Islam and Christianity. Such a world Faith will, in the end, overwhelm such prejudice and hate with love.

Christ was a Jew, born among the Jews, but Christianity is an independent religion though it was first called a sect of Judaism.

Buddha was born among the Hindus, but His religion, Buddhism, was an independent religion though it was thought for a long time to be a sect of Hinduism.

Bahá'u'lláh was born among the Muslims, but His religion, the Bahá'í Faith, is an independent religion no

matter how loudly and angrily the enemies of the Bahá'í
Faith in Iran describe it as a sect – subversive, dangerous,
and worthy of death.

Dr Raymond Frank Piper, not a Bahá'í, while a
member of the Philosophy Department of Syracuse
University in New York State, said: 'The Bahá'í teachings
are providentially loaded with precisely the goods which
we direly need in this catastrophic era.'

Dr Piper described the Bahá'í Faith as 'one of the
noblest of the world's religions.'

Not noblest *sect*, noblest *religion*.

He added this about the Bahá'ís and their religion:

> They [the Bahá'ís] have long set their wills to attain
> those world institutions which we are just now finding
> indispensable for peace. The Bahá'í teachings can
> contribute immensely, I believe, to that training for
> world citizenship which we sorely need. The amazing
> fitness of these teachings to our needs and their peculiar
> timeliness are two facts which attest their divine origin.

There is an entire publication called *Appreciations of
the Bahá'í Faith*. It is a tribute to the fellowship, love and
unity which the Bahá'í religion brings into the world.

Former President of Czechoslovakia, Eduard Beneš,
not a Bahá'í, said of the Bahá'í Faith that it was 'one of
the spiritual forces now absolutely necessary to put the
spirit first in this battle against material forces'. He added:
'The Bahá'í teaching is one of the great instruments for
the final victory of the spirit and of humanity.'

There is a secondary charge made in this accusation,
stating that the Bahá'í Faith wishes to set up its own
regime in Iran and overthrow the government.

You have already heard the refutation of that absurd
accusation. No Bahá'í, and no Bahá'í institution, could
ever participate in such a violent 'subversive' action. Such
intolerable behaviour is *forbidden* in the writings of the
Bahá'í Faith.

Anyone who has even the slightest knowledge about the Bahá'í Faith and its teachings would recognize that the charge is not only fraudulent, but laughable.

However, out of respect for those who may not yet know very much about this world religion, let me once again turn to a source outside the Bahá'í Faith as a further answer to this baseless charge.

When this same accusation was made during the regime of the late Shah, at the time of the terrible persecutions of Bahá'ís in Iran in 1955, Dr Hugh van Rensselaer of Brooklyn College, a highly-respected educator, not a Bahá'í, answered it clearly and succinctly. He came to the aid of the Bahá'ís who were being persecuted during those hideous days of 1955, not as a supporter of the Bahá'í Faith, but as a lover of mankind. He spoke against all persecution, writing of the Bahá'ís:

> My purpose in saying this is not to save the Bahá'í adherents from suffering – although no kind-hearted person desires to see anyone suffer. Rather, my purpose is to save Iran from making upon the world an impression of being uncivilized. The stories about a Bahá'í threat to set up a Bahá'í regime in Iran are no more convincing than were the German stories about the Jews and about the Poles when Hitler wanted an excuse to persecute Jews and Poles. The stories sound like the inventions of men who wish to have a pretext, even if it is a fictitious pretext, to justify their persecutions. This is not civilized.

It wasn't 'civilized' in 1955, it is not 'civilized' in 1981. Persecution, assassination, murder, arson, looting, kidnapping and illegal executions will never be 'civilized'. A century and a half of it is barbaric.

Accusation refuted!

The well-known and gifted French columnist, Eric Rouleau, pointed out in his column in *Le Monde* that three of the most common accusations made against the Bahá'í community in Iran these days come under the headings:

The Shah, the United States, and *Israel*

Under these three headings, persistent, baseless charges have been deliberately repeated over and over, with variations, in the media of both Europe and North America, wherever representatives of the present regime in Iran are on television and radio or in the press.

Therefore, I shall deal with them now, one at a time, as promised earlier, and will expose these misrepresentations and the fraudulent nature of these accusations once and for all.

Let us deal first with Reza Shah.

ACCUSATION

The Bahá'ís supported the Pahlavi Shah's regime and were favoured by his government.

One of the great ironies of the situation in Iran is the way in which the basic Bahá'í principle of loyalty and obedience to whatever government is in power has been traduced and used against the Bahá'ís. Because the Bahá'ís did not oppose the Shah, therefore they supported him! In fact, some of the worst pogroms they have suffered took place under the Pahlavis. Successive regimes made the same dishonest charges. For instance, even now the opponents of Ayatollah Khomeini are accusing the Bahá'ís of supporting him, just because they do not engage in active opposition. This baseless charge is often used in Iran today as a pretext to beat, harass, and all too often kill the Bahá'ís.

THE TRUTH

From the time of its birth in 1844, under a succession of

hostile regimes, the Bahá'ís received no legal recognition, had no place to appeal against injustices, and suffered from repeated pogroms. This did not change with the appearance of the Pahlavi regime. The father of Muhammad Reza Shah came to power in 1921 through a *coup d'état*, although he was not recognized as Shah until 1925. Anti-government riots were not uncommon during these years. The Bahá'ís were in no way involved but, as has been the case throughout the history of these persecutions, they became the scapegoats.

The brief report which follows is but one leaf, from one tree, from an entire forest of oppression suffered by the Bahá'í community in Iran under every regime in its turn. This includes the regime of the late Shah.

We mention here only the most flagrant abuses, and only a part of those. To tell the full story would require a thick volume and neither of us has either the time or the taste for that.

Violent attacks were made against the Bahá'ís in Jahrum in 1926. Several were killed. Although the authorities did not instigate these dreadful persecutions directly, they did nothing to protect the Bahá'ís, nor did they interfere with their persecutors and murderers. No one was ever punished for any of the murders in Jahrum. No one was even questioned.*

BAHÁ'Í WORLD COMMUNITY APPEALS TO
REZA SHAH PAHLAVI AGAINST THE PERSECU-
TION OF THE BAHÁ'ÍS

Your Majesty: Moved by the cruel persecutions being inflicted upon the Bahá'ís of Persia, we address this petition to [you as] the supreme authority of that land, confident that when all the facts are assembled, the con-

---

* See *The Bábí and Bahá'í Religions, 1844–1944,* ed. by Moojan Momen (George Ronald, Oxford, 1981), pp. 465–72, for an account of this episode.

ditions realized and the consequences understood, Your Majesty will straightway initiate whatever measures are necessary to terminate this long and frightful chapter of unmerited woe.

This appeal, which appeared in the press in 1926, was made on behalf of the Bahá'í World Community to the Shah, supreme head of the Pahlavi regime which the Bahá'ís today are accused of supporting.

The king turned a deaf ear.

The appeal included these words:

On that day eight Bahá'ís were tortured and slain under circumstances of unbelievable brutality . . . In addition to those murdered outright, many [other Bahá'ís] were severely wounded, and some twenty houses overrun and looted, or burned to the ground.

Among the atrocious acts committed in Jahrum, was the slaughter of Bahá'í women in the most shameful manner, and the cutting into pieces of the body of a Bahá'í child . . .

The refusal to help was an example of the 'favours' which the Bahá'ís received from the Pahlavi regime from beginning to end.

These bestial persecutions of the Bahá'ís were repeated with varying degrees of intensity and ferocity during the entire reigns of the two Pahlavi Shahs: 1925, 1930–32, 1934, 1939–40, 1941, 1943–50, and 1955.

In the years between 1943 and 1950, several Bahá'í Centres were confiscated. Some were destroyed.

Bahá'ís were imprisoned in Kashan and Sharud.

Bahá'ís were assassinated in different parts of the country.

No attempt of any kind was made by the government to apprehend the murderers. Somehow, the 'favours' of the regime of Muhammad Reza Shah became 'mixed up', and, whether intentional or unintentional, the 'favours' went to the *slaughterers,* and not to the *slain.*

A massive, venomous campaign, unequalled in ferocity and savagery, was launched against the Bahá'ís in Iran in 1955. As usual, it was the clergy who served as the spearhead.

One of the leading priests publicly denounced the Bahá'í Faith as a 'false religion'. He preached daily in the mosques. He was supported by the government of Muhammad Reza Shah, for both the national and the Army radio stations broadcast his vitriolic sermons throughout the entire country, uninterruptedly day after day. This leading mulla aroused the hatred of the illiterate masses to a fever pitch of fury against the Bahá'ís.

On April 21, 1955, the Army surrounded the Bahá'í National Centre in Teheran while Bahá'í delegates from all parts of the country were gathered for their Annual Convention.

On May 7, the building was occupied by troops.

As a climax, in August high-ranking officers of the Shah's Army and eminent dignitaries of the clergy arrived with great ceremony. They were to have the honour of administering the first pickaxe blows against the beautiful dome of the Bahá'í National Centre. Together, they would participate in the demolition of that symbol of the Bahá'í Faith they all hated.

In those days of crisis of 1955, the Minister of the Interior announced in the Iranian Parliament that the Government of Muhammad Reza Shah had issued orders for the suppression of the hated 'Bahá'í Sect'.

This occasioned a fresh outburst of violence and bloodshed. A wave of murders, rapes and robberies against the Bahá'í community took place across the entire country. Bahá'í women were violated. Bahá'í girls were abducted and forced into marriage with Muslims. Children were expelled from their schools.

The House of the Báb, site of pilgrimage for the Bahá'ís

of the world, was ruined. Its entire structure was severely damaged. Its rooms were turned into rubble.

Bahá'í cemeteries were desecrated. Graves were opened. The corpses of the Bahá'í dead were disinterred, mutilated and scattered in a country-wide display of ghoulish depravity.

No one objected.

Except the Bahá'ís.

The Bahá'í International Community mounted a vigorous, world-wide campaign. Cablegrams and telegrams poured in from all over the world to the Shah, his Prime Minister and Parliament. Help was sought from the United Nations, from the Presidents and heads of various countries, and from leading humanitarian organizations in all parts of the world.

Faced with the serious situation of an impending nation-wide massacre of Bahá'ís, the Secretary-General of the United Nations, Mr Dag Hammarskjöld, sent his representative to the head of the Iranian delegation to the United Nations.

The increasing strength of the international opposition being massed against Iran at length compelled the Government of the Shah to listen. It brought to a halt the outward persecutions. Gradually, reluctantly, most of the confiscated Bahá'í properties were returned.

On the part of Iran it was a cease-fire in the face of world opinion. On the part of the Bahá'ís, it was another temporary breathing-spell.

Despite the assurances given to the world by the Government of the Shah, the Bahá'ís continued to be the object of all kinds of behind-the-scenes abuses. The persecutions now became clandestine. As far as the world was concerned, outwardly all seemed to be well. Only the Bahá'ís knew that the same old deprivation of human rights was now being carried out surreptitiously, but just as relentlessly. Everything was quiet, but unchanged.

This state of quiescence did not last long.

Soon Bahá'í gatherings were disrupted by the Army. Bahá'í meetings were finally banned. Homes were searched. Pressure was brought to bear on employers of Bahá'ís to dismiss them.

The momentum in 1956 gradually but inexorably moved toward another possible climax of terror. The Bahá'í International Community, fearing a renewed outbreak of violent hostility, appealed once more to the United Nations.

Dr José Vincent Trujillo, delegate of Ecuador and President of the Economic and Social Council, brought the case of the Bahá'ís to the attention of the Special Commission for the Prevention of Discrimination and Protection of Minorities.

The Commission was successful in putting an end to these renewed, flagrant violations of the Charter of Human Rights. After all, the Commission pointed out, Iran was a signatory to that Charter.

The Government of Iran, as far as the persecution of the Bahá'ís was concerned, in the face of the threat of renewed world publicity, 'went underground' again.

But not very deep. And only temporarily.

The Shah's regime continued to practise, through the clergy, as much oppression of the Bahá'í community as might escape the detection of world opinion, yet still let the Bahá'ís know where they stood.

The Bahá'ís were deeply grateful to the Secretary-General, Dag Hammarskjöld, and to Dr Trujillo and the Special Commission. They were, however, because of nearly a hundred and fifty years of experience, dubious about the lasting effects of any cessation of persecution against them.

Their fears were well founded.

Bahá'ís are instructed by Bahá'u'lláh, the Founder of their Faith, to remember that they must live among their fellow men so that their whole life is a prayer. Their daily work, whatever it may be, when carried out to the very best of their ability, and in service to their fellow men, when performed with skill, trust and integrity, is the very finest kind of prayer.

Everyone wants an employee like that, even enemies; although in Iran, they may have to kill them later on, if the clergy insist.

The head of National Airlines, Iran Air, and some in other high administrative positions, were Bahá'ís. They could be trusted and depended upon to put the welfare of their country before their own. A rare, precious, and almost vanished virtue.

Because of their integrity and honour, because of the positions of trust which they have held, Bahá'ís have been accused of being supporters of whatever regime it was that employed them. But they were simply employees who could be trusted to do their best for king and country without ever compromising their own Bahá'í principles. The jobs they undertook were never political.

The trust and integrity of the Bahá'í merchants is clearly described in the book written by the United States Supreme Court Justice, William O. Douglas, *West of the Indus**. Douglas says:

> The Baha'is have many businessmen among their numbers. They enjoy a fine reputation as merchants. The reason is that they maintain a high ethical standard in all their dealings. Merchants in the bazaar are quick to take advantage; they will cheat and palm off false or inferior goods. Never the Baha'is. They are scrupulous in their dealings; and as a result they grow in prestige.

No wonder the Bahá'ís were sought out as employees. Whatever the positions of trust they might hold, they would not do anything contrary to the welfare of the Persian people or of the nation. Nor would they do

* Doubleday & Company, New York, 1958.

anything that would dishonour or degrade the holy name
of their Faith.

They would die first. Many have.

Under the rule of Muhammad Reza Shah another
attempt, from an entirely different angle, was made to
obliterate the Bahá'í Faith from the land. This time, it was
done by a proposal to erase from the history books all
historical events involving the Faith and even any
mention of it. The Shah offered no opposition to this
plan, designed to make it appear as though the Bahá'í
Faith had never existed in Iran. This silence was another
of his 'favours'.

Widespread and ruthless assaults on an innocent
people took place not only with the blessing of the clergy,
but with the open encouragement of the Shah's Government. The philosophy had always been clear: Better that
the mobs should attack the Bahá'ís and enjoy some sport,
rather than revolt against a government in trouble. As one
local fanatic among the religious authorities said, quite
frankly:

'That's what Bahá'ís are for.'

Finally, we come to the photograph.

It tells better than any words exactly how much the
Bahá'í community of Iran 'supported' the Shah and his
Army. It also demonstrates yet again the 'favours' which
that same Shah bestowed upon the Bahá'ís.

In 1955 when the news first arrived about the destruction of the beautiful dome of the Bahá'í National Centre
in Teheran, the Bahá'ís were told that 'unruly' and
'uncontrollable' mobs were responsible for the first attack.

It soon became apparent that the Army had occupied
the Bahá'í property on behalf of the Government and in
support of the fanatical clergy.

It is true that mobs, out of control, incited by the clergy,
were seizing, looting, and often burning Bahá'í Centres
and homes in every part of the country that year. Day in
and day out, hour after hour, inflammatory sermons were

Destruction of the dome of the Bahá'í National Centre, led by high-ranking Army officers, Teheran, 1955

being broadcast by the radio stations of Iran, arousing the mobs against the Bahá'ís.

Unfortunately for the destroyers, photographs were taken of their personal participation in the destruction of the Bahá'í National Centre in Teheran. They were proud of what they were doing to the Bahá'ís. But in their pleasure and gratification, they entirely overlooked world opinion and how foolish they would appear as high-ranking Generals taking a pickaxe to a sacred religious building.

I was in Africa reading the stories about these 'uncontrollable' mobs. At the same time, I was also holding in my hand the photograph which you have just seen. Two of the 'uncontrollable mob' were wearing the uniforms of Generals in the Army of Muhammad Reza Shah. One was Chief of the General Staff, the other Chief of Security.

What was this 'uncontrollable' mob of two doing?

They were taking turns, with a pickaxe, to destroy the beautiful dome of the Bahá'í National Centre on Shiraz Avenue in the capital city. More than that. One can easily see from the gleeful facial expressions exactly how sad they felt about having to do such a dreadful thing.

But duty is duty.

Far from 'supporting' or collaborating with the regime of the Shah, contrary to being 'favoured' by it, the Bahá'í community in Iran suffered constantly, continuously and ruthlessly from both Pahlavi opposition and oppression, as well as from silence and indifference to their many appeals for justice.

Mark the charge: Refuted.

ACCUSATION

The Bahá'ís are agents of foreign powers.

'Roll the Drums! Sound the Trumpets! Tyrant Loose!' In the accompanying illustration you can see a greatly

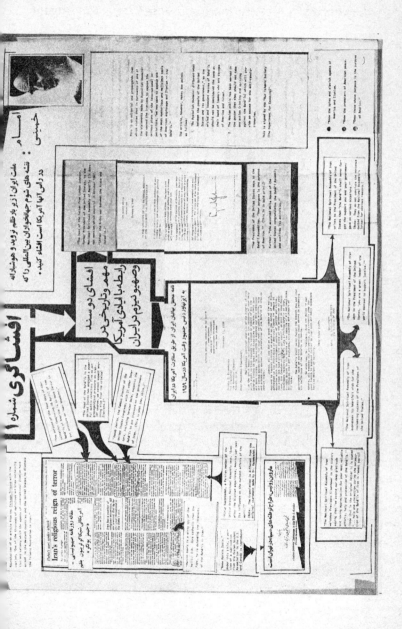

reduced version, with partial English translation and comments, of the large inflammatory poster which the enemies of the Bahá'í community in Iran have been displaying throughout that country. You have already heard most of the misrepresentations and false charges it contains. The report you have just read on the regime of the Shah has dealt with most of them.

The important thing to consider on this poster are the copies of two letters concerning former Presidents of the United States, General Dwight D. Eisenhower and Lyndon B. Johnson.

The letters have been put before the people of Iran to arouse them against the Bahá'ís. It gives the authorities another chance to make the same fraudulent charge that Bahá'ís are agents for a foreign power – in this case the United States.

THE TRUTH

President Eisenhower was a friend of Iran; he came to visit that country. The Bahá'í community there, in company with many more organizations, not Bahá'í, welcomed him in friendly fashion. The copy of their courteous letter to the President was reproduced from the American *Bahá'í News* and is in the centre of the poster.

To the present regime, this letter is clear evidence of 'spies' at work. In truth, the Bahá'í community in Iran had far more reason than any other organization in that land to write such a letter of welcome and thanks to President Eisenhower.

What the poster also fails to tell you, is the story of the many futile appeals for help which the Bahá'í community in Iran made in 1955 to Muhammad Reza Shah, to his Government, and to the high-ranking members of the clergy, any of whom were in a position to help. All refused. Repeatedly.

Having failed to secure any help or protection from the authorities, the Bahá'í World Community (not the Bahá'í community in Iran), as a last resort, launched an appeal to the United Nations, to governments, and to men of goodwill everywhere. President Eisenhower was among them.

He was not alone.

The same appeal was lodged with the Secretary-General of the United Nations, and with the President of the Economic and Social Council. Copies of it were delivered to the representatives of the member nations of that Council, to the Director of the Human Rights Commission, as well as to all non-governmental organizations with consultative status. Every avenue of assistance was explored in the face of Iran's complete and icy indifference. Gradually, the whole world became aware of the terror that reigned in the streets of Iran in 1955.

Reports such as the following finally led to concerted international action. Here are some excerpts from Press reports:

Shops, farms and homes plundered throughout Iran.
Crops burned, livestock slaughtered, owners evicted.
Bodies in various cemeteries throughout the country disinterred and viciously mutilated.
Children and adults beaten on the streets.
Children mobbed at school and expelled.
Young women abducted and compelled against both their own and parents' wishes to marry Muslims.
Teen-aged girl shamelessly raped.
Eleven-month-old-baby deliberately trampled under foot.
All Bahá'ís ordered to recant or be killed.

The reports became ever more alarming and violent. It was the following tragic story which finally started the wheels rolling in high places. People of the civilized world were shocked, but were still reluctant to believe that in the year 1955 these atrocities could be happening in a country signatory to the United Nations Declaration on Human

Rights. They changed their minds when the following report came from Iran.

BRUTAL FAMILY MASSACRE

Emboldened by general applause and official approval which accompanied recent killings of Bahá'ís, wholesale destruction of their property, mobs began to look for victims in more remote areas.

Today a mob of many hundreds marched upon the hamlet of Hurmuzak. To the beating of drums and the sound of trumpets, armed with spades and axes, they fell in a swarm upon a family of seven, oldest eighty, youngest nineteen. In an orgy of unrestrained fanaticism, the mob literally hacked the entire family to pieces.*

Almost every organization, and every individual who arose to denounce the persecutions of 1955, voiced the same words of shock, incredulity and disbelief.

Author and educator, Harry A. Overstreet, not a Bahá'í, declared: 'Many of us in the western world think of the Bahá'í Faith as one of the great contributions to the culture and sanity of the world.'

The famous Oxford scholar, Gilbert Murray, wrote in a letter to the Editor of the *Manchester Guardian*, August 22, 1955: 'A country such as Iran, whose Government approved the Declaration on Human Rights, can ill-afford to permit fanatics to attack with violence the peaceful followers of a harmless and progressive religion.'

The *Manchester Guardian* in its August 13 issue of that year carried this statement in a leading article: 'The Persian Government will harm itself in the world's eyes if it allows the persecution of the Bahá'ís to continue.'

Professor Pitirim A. Sorokin of Harvard University

---

* This episode is fully described in *The Seven Martyrs of Hurmuzak*, by Muḥammad Labíb, translated and with a Foreword by Moojan Momen (George Ronald, Oxford, 1981).

REFUTATION 43

wrote a most helpful letter of protest to the Iranian
Embassy in Washington during those same horrendous
persecutions.

> Such persecution of this highly spiritual and moral
> religion appears to me to be entirely unjustifiable and
> incomprehensible. I hope that the government of Iran
> will have sufficient moral and religious responsibility
> and just common sense to stop this sort of persecution. I
> have no doubt that the impression which Iran is now
> creating upon the rest of the world should be of some
> concern to all those who are in a position to stop all
> persecution upon those of the Bahá'í Faith.

As you can see, the President was not alone.

None of these men of goodwill responded because they
were supporting the Bahá'í Faith. They acted on behalf of
humanity because they were against genocide and persecution in all its ugly forms.

Revolted by these same injustices, President Dwight D.
Eisenhower made a forceful and courageous request to
the Government of Muhammad Reza Shah to cease such
persecutions at once. The President considered it uncivi-
lized.

Fearing that massacres might follow in other parts, the
United Nations took immediate action with the representatives of Iran. Through the skill and diplomacy of its
Secretary-General and his aides, the waves of persecution
were brought to an end.

At least to the gaze of the outer world.

Peace in Iran was apparently restored.

Only the Bahá'ís knew that the persecution of their
community had gone underground. Temporarily. Until it
was wise and safe to surface again.

They knew it would be soon.

Who would believe that a nation such as Iran would
wish to face international scorn and scandal a second
time? Who would believe that in such a short time

persecutions even more vicious than those of 1955 would break out once again?

Only the Bahá'ís would believe it.

A new regime, a new reign of terror, another try at extermination. It had never ended. Would it ever end?

Obviously each new regime in Iran believes it can do better than the previous one. They prefer to make their own mistakes. The present one seems not to care whether the rest of the world is looking or not.

The Bahá'ís were not the only ones sceptical about the sincerity and integrity of the present regime in Iran on matters of human rights. When, at that regime's request, the United Nations sent a Committee to investigate the human rights record of the late Shah, the columnist, Jack Anderson, made a few suggestions.

During his segment on the WABC-TV programme, 'Good Morning America', Mr Anderson suggested that the international investigators, while they were in Iran, should also investigate the human rights abuses of the present regime.

Savak, he pointed out, are gone, but 'a new secret police, Savama, are operating with impunity. They arrest political opponents just like Savak used to do. Phones are tapped, letters are intercepted, persecution is rampant. Little seems changed.'

Hundreds of people, he continued, who are thought to be opponents of the head of the present regime are ordered executed. Accused at the whim of, and 'convicted by the Revolutionary Courts seeking revenge, not justice.'

Bahá'ís too, the broadcast pointed out, are living in terror. They have been hounded and harassed. Their religious shrines have been 'desecrated'.

Liberation, in its edition of December 8, 1980, referred to the 'mischievous' and unjust actions of one of the most highly-placed religious leaders of Iran. During a trial in Mahabad, this high-ranking divine spotted a tradesman he knew was a Bahá'í. The Bahá'í was one of the witnesses. The religious leader interrupted the trial. The opportunity was too good to miss. He summoned the Bahá'í to his presence and told him that he must deny his religion immediately.

The Bahá'í refused.

He was ordered to pay a considerable sum of money, or to deny his Faith. That was the choice. The divine, renowned in judicial circles, judged the Bahá'í on the spot, and deemed him worthy of being shot to death for his double refusal.

He would not deny his Faith, nor would he pay a bribe. It was only the century-and-a-half-old game played all over again.

'Recant.'

'Never!'

'Free yourself by paying a ransom.'

'Never!'

On September 27, 1979, in the town of Mahabad, Mr Bahár Vujdání paid the price of this injustice with his life. Mr Vujdání is on my honour roll.

If you want to know the name of the legal assassin, it's easy. You know the date and the city, look it up. Every Bahá'í in Iran knows it, and their fellow Bahá'ís now know, all over the world.

The assassin is free. No one can touch him. He has a high murder immunity. And talent for it.

Such an *individual* killer let loose upon the streets of any big city of the world would be called psychotic. The police of every major city would at once call for an APB, *All Points Broadcast*: 'Killer loose. Armed. Dangerous.'

Unfortunately, in Iran, these *are* the police.

I said that.

Now you know why the Bahá'í community of Iran was courteous enough, and grateful enough, to say 'Thank you' and 'Welcome!' when President Eisenhower came to their country.

How could you not be thankful to one who had helped

you escape such horrible persecutions and death – even temporarily.

You won't find this part of that story anywhere on that fraudulent poster. But now you know why they hated the President for helping their 'quarry' escape yet another time.

The second letter referring to a President of the United States is one from President Lyndon B. Johnson. The authorities in Iran describe it as coming from the 'accursed White House'.

President Johnson is writing to the National Spiritual Assembly of the Bahá'ís of the United States on behalf of the entire Bahá'í World Community. He is congratulating them on the occasion of the one hundredth anniversary of the proclamation of Bahá'u'lláh's Faith to the world with its message of love and unity for all mankind. In the President's own words:

'Yours has been a work of love. You have sown seeds of righteousness and justice, and humanity will reap rich harvests from your toil.'

President Johnson, at the end of his letter, declares:

'All thoughtful and farsighted men respect the mission of your faith.'

He then refers to Bahá'u'lláh's own words, saying that 'every one of us looks forward to that day when the earth will truly be one country and mankind its citizens.'

All that is on the poster. Real 'spy' talk!

President Lyndon B. Johnson made the grave mistake of saying that such purposes as world peace and world unity were the purposes of men of goodwill everywhere, including the United States of America.

Hence the present authorities in Iran, having vandalized the Bahá'í Centre, and stolen all the documents, came upon this one. With their customary brilliant analysis, they perverted the meaning of this letter to imply that the Bahá'ís and the United States Government have one and the same 'purpose': To destroy Iran!

If all the Heads of State, Presidents, Prime Ministers, Senators, Congressmen, leading figures in Parliaments, Education and the Arts, who expressed the same 'congratulations' to the Bahá'í Faith on that occasion, in countries all over the world, were to be given a place on that poster, it would be covered entirely to an even greater number of levels than before.

Thus do love, friendship and fellowship swamp anger, hatred and revenge, and in the end, to the maddening frustration of the malevolent, will win out.

In reality, the poster should be covered with the photographs of the humanitarians and goodwill ambassadors of love and unity who helped the Bahá'ís during those dark days, but since it was only President Dwight D. Eisenhower and President Lyndon B. Johnson who made it to the poster of hate, I offer the following suggestion:

The entire poster should be blank except for two large photographs of President Eisenhower and President Johnson, very large and in the centre.

Underneath their pictures, in huge letters, written on behalf of men of goodwill everywhere, should be the words:

'Bravo!'

Mark the charge: Refuted.

ACCUSATION

The Bahá'ís are 'spies' for Israel, and secretly collaborate with international Zionism. They contribute financially to the support of Israel which aids that country against its Arab and Muslim neighbours.

The full story of the relationship of the Bahá'í Faith to Israel, and to Iran, Islam, and the peoples of the world, is beautiful, dramatic and thrilling. But we shall deal only with the false and baseless charges made against the Bahá'í Faith by the present regime in Iran. We shall demonstrate once again how utterly fraudulent and absurd their charges are.

Had they received the proper counsel, they would surely have been told: 'Don't make them. They will be exploded, and you will look foolish in the eyes of the world.'

So be it.

One of their baseless charges is that the Bahá'í Faith sends funds regularly to Israel to support the alliance between the Bahá'ís and Zionism.

THE TRUTH

All money sent to the Bahá'í World Centre by the Bahá'ís of the world, including those in Iran, is contributed solely and exclusively for the upkeep of their Holy Shrines and historic sites, and for the administration of their Faith.

The followers of other religions likewise support their own Holy Places and administrative offices situated in Israel. This includes contributions offered by Muslims for the upkeep and repairs of the Al-Aqsa Mosque in Jerusalem.

Israel is a land of four world religions: Judaism, Christianity, Islam and the Bahá'í Faith. All have holy places there.

Furthermore, it is a basic principle of the Bahá'í Faith that Bahá'í institutions do not and cannot accept contributions from non-Bahá'ís, whether individuals, institutions or governments.

Thus, the Bahá'í World Centre, unlike Jewish, Christian and Muslim religious institutions in Israel which apply for and receive government subsidies for the upkeep of their religious endowments, does not accept, as a matter of principle, any such subsidies from the Government of Israel.

The Bahá'í Faith maintains itself and its properties

solely from the financial assistance it receives from the members of the Bahá'í Faith in all lands.

If the contributions made by poor and rich alike to the upkeep of the Bahá'í Faith are wrong, if the sacrifices made by these dear souls for the religion they love are improper, then the present regime in Iran should immediately stop all contributions made by Muslims to the upkeep of their own Shrines and historical sites and penalize severely such acts of Iranian treachery by their own people, forbidding also such contributions by members of the Jewish, Christian and Zoroastrian religions.

Of course, it's ridiculous.

What else?

ACCUSATION

The Bahá'í Faith has its World Centre in Israel. This choice shows that the Bahá'ís are supporters of international Zionism, and are hostile to the Islamic nations and Arab neighbours of Israel.

THE TRUTH

What the enemies of the Bahá'í Faith in Iran totally ignore is a simple fact of history which makes this particular 'accusation' even more ridiculous than the others.

Why is the Bahá'í World Centre in Israel? And why are its holy Shrines located in Israel?

The World Administrative Centre of the Bahá'í Faith was established in the Holy Land because of historical events which occurred more than half a century *before* the establishment of the State of Israel.

Bahá'u'lláh was sent as an exile and a prisoner to the Holy Land. He had no choice of His destination. He was banished there by a decree of Sultan Abdul-Aziz, the ruler of the Islamic Ottoman Empire. The partner in His harsh exile was the Government of Iran, the accuser.

For the remainder of His life, Bahá'u'lláh was a prisoner. He passed away near 'Akká in 1892 in what, fifty-six years later, became the State of Israel.

Even more astonishing and absurd in the face of these baseless charges is the fact that the prime mover in Bahá'u'lláh's exiles, which terminated in the Holy Land, was the Government of Iran, the predecessors of these very authorities who today are now complaining because the Bahá'ís are there.

Ironic, isn't it?

The 'accusation' that the Bahá'í Faith is 'hostile' to *any* nation is equally false.

The Bahá'í Faith has no enmity for any nation, people, or creed. It does not take sides in political controversies. It does not side with one nation against another nation. Such a practice or policy would be completely contrary to the Bahá'í principle of the oneness of mankind, and would be directly opposed to its most fundamental teachings.

For Bahá'ís, as promoters of genuine love for all mankind, and as proclaimers of the oneness of humanity, taking sides in such disputes would be diametrically opposed to their most basic religious beliefs. Their basic goals for the union of all the peoples of the world would become a mockery. The purpose of the Bahá'í Faith has always been the peace, prosperity, security, and freedom of every nation. Every country should develop its own special qualities, talents, language and culture without infringing on the rights and privileges of any other nation.

Imagine the ridiculous position in which this puts the present authorities in Iran. They are prepared to denounce, persecute and kill the Bahá'ís because they are Zionists (false), who have taken sides with the enemies of Islamic nations (false), and because the Bahá'í World Centre is in Israel, a fact which their predecessors made inevitable by forcing Bahá'u'lláh along His route of banishment from His native Iran. That exile led Him to the prison-city of 'Akka, and to the side of Mount Carmel, the Vineyard of God, fulfilling prophecies from all the holy Books of the past, including the sacred writings of Islam.

That *accusation* is not only *refuted,* it was silly of them to bring it up in the first place.

ACCUSATION

The Bahá'ís of Iran have been acting as 'spies' for Israel, travelling back and forth carrying and bringing information to be used against Iran.

THE TRUTH

Bahá'ís *do* travel to Israel, from all parts of the world, including Iran. At least they did travel to Israel from Iran before the present cruel restrictions against Iranian Bahá'í Pilgrimages were applied.

But there wasn't one 'spy' among them.

What the Bahá'ís of Iran were bringing to Israel from their country were hearts full of love and prayers. They returned to Iran with the same hearts overflowing with joy and happiness. The experiences and lessons learned in Israel at their holy Shrines inspired them and made them more determined than ever to become finer human beings, better persons.

They were on 'Pilgrimage' to the Holy Shrines of their Faith.

If such a sin merits persecution and death, and should be stopped, what a shock it is going to be to their *own* people who make regular pilgrimages to Qum and Mashhad and to Mecca and Medina.

Christians must cease going to Bethlehem and Nazareth.

I think the point is painfully clear, the absurdity self-evident, and the falseness of the charge childish.

In a land such as Iran, where Bahá'ís are deprived of

legal and human rights, one cannot expect to be granted spiritual rights, such as the joys of pilgrimage. In Iran, if you are a Bahá'í, you can expect that even such a beautiful, sacred and holy thing as the pilgrimage will be perverted. They will try in every way to spoil and misrepresent it.

Now we come to the nub of it all.

ACCUSATION

The Bahá'ís are enemies of Islam and its Prophet Muhammad.

THE TRUTH

They are not.

Let it be stated clearly and without any 'buts' or 'ifs', that the Bahá'í Faith recognizes the Prophet Muhammad as the Apostle of God and regards His book, the Koran, as the Word of God. This is an article of faith to all Bahá'ís, who, through the teachings of Bahá'u'lláh, have learned to love and revere Muhammad and to recognize with awe and wonder the great role which His religion, Islam, has played in human history.

The actions of Muslims and Muslim governments today are no better standard by which to judge Islam than are the materialism and permissiveness and disorderliness of Christian countries a standard by which to judge Christianity.

Muhammad Himself said there should be 'no compulsion in religion'. (Koran 2:257)

The clergy and regime in Iran today, 1981, say: 'Recant your religion and become Muslims, or die.'

The Bahá'í teaching of the oneness of *all* religions is given in chapter 13. You can see in one glance there, in the two drawings, why a Bahá'í could never be an enemy of any one of them; it would mean being an enemy of

Bahá'u'lláh and the Bahá'í Faith, an enemy of *all* religions, an enemy of God Himself.

ACCUSATION

Some leading political figures in Iran have been Bahá'ís, including a Prime Minister.

THE TRUTH

None has ever been a Bahá'í.

In 1965, Mr Abbas Hoveida became Prime Minister.

Immediately, his political opponents accused him of being a Bahá'í. It is a favourite device.

Politicians in Iran have used this 'ploy' whenever it seemed useful. The Bahá'ís suffer because of it. That has been one of the 'fringe benefits' for the enemy.

These accusations, charging the Bahá'ís with corrupt political activities, and even declaring that they have served in high political office, are still being deliberately spread. They are, of course, false.

They do it for two reasons:

1. To discredit their political opponents who have been prominent or might rise to a position of power. By associating their names with the Bahá'í Faith, they hope to weaken this threat to their own prestige.
2. To incite further hatred against the Bahá'ís from the fanatical sections of the population who fear it might be true, and who dread having Bahá'ís come into any position of influence in the country. It is intolerable to them.

It shows how little they know about or understand the character of Bahá'ís and the integrity of their service to their country. Although Bahá'ís do not participate in party politics, it is true that whenever they serve in administrative or non-political positions in governments, they acquire reputations for honesty, truthfulness and trustworthiness. To be called a Bahá'í administrator would be considered a compliment almost anywhere but in Iran.

The present regime in Iran is still repeating the same old false charge that Mr Abbas Hoveida was a Bahá'í. It is done for the inflammatory purposes already mentioned. This false allegation stems from the fact that his grandfather was a Bahá'í in the time of Bahá'u'lláh, and his father was a member of the Bahá'í Faith for some time.

However, when the father accepted a political assignment in the Foreign Ministry of Iran, he no longer remained a member of the Bahá'í community.

Mr Hoveida himself never became a Bahá'í.

He, himself, repeatedly and emphatically asserted that he was a Muslim.

In order to make certain that everybody *knew* he was *not* a Bahá'í, Mr Hoveida began, during his term of office, to create many hardships and difficulties for the Bahá'í community in Iran.

During his regime, many Bahá'í homes were burned and looted. Many Bahá'ís were dismissed from their administrative posts in government simply because they *were* Bahá'ís.

This is the true story behind these false accusations that leading figures in the political government of Iran have been Bahá'ís.

These are baseless charges, like all the others.

Another Minister, Mansur Rawhani, whose father was a Bahá'í and whose mother was a Muslim, has been described by his political enemies as a Bahá'í.

He was not. He had never been a Bahá'í.

ACCUSATION

The Bahá'ís of Iran are quite different from those in other lands. In Iran they are politically oriented.

THE TRUTH

Whenever you hear the name of a Bahá'í mentioned as part of the political process in Iran, or anywhere else, be sure the statement is false.

Absolutely and categorically.

Should a Bahá'í ever wish to take part in political ventures, and proceed to carry out that desire, he would be immediately removed from the Bahá'í community.

Mark the Charge: Refuted.

ACCUSATION

Bahá'ís have been members of the dreaded secret police of Muhammad Reza Shah, the notorious Savak. A Bahá'í was at one time head of this organization, and Bahá'ís were members of other departments.

THE TRUTH

This accusation, like that concerning the Prime Minister, is completely false. Its purpose is the same, to try to discredit the Bahá'í Faith internationally in the eyes of the world and, locally, to inflame and enrage the people of Iran against the Bahá'ís.

In September 1978, during the present four-year-long wave of persecution, Savak, the Shah's special police, organized a powerful anti-Bahá'í movement in Shiraz, the birthplace of the Herald of the Bahá'í Faith, the Báb, and the city in which the Bahá'í Faith began.

The purpose of this sudden violent attack by Savak was to discredit publicly the revolutionary clergy by laying the blame on them, but the mullas learned of their intention and on this occasion intervened on behalf of the Bahá'ís.

Over three hundred Bahá'í homes were burned to get Savak's campaign of terror and extermination off to a good start. No one knew at the outset where these attacks would lead, how violently they would develop, or how widespread and sinister they would become.

There is no way to link the Bahá'í Faith to that dreaded organization, Savak.

As in the case of the ex-Prime Minister, Mr Hoveida, the accusation that the late head of Savak, General Nasiri, as well as some other officials, such as Parviz Sabeti, were Bahá'ís, is utterly false. They have never been Bahá'ís, although other members of their families may have been.

It is a basic principle of the Bahá'í religion that the gift of faith springs from the free choice of the individual. The Bahá'í Faith cannot be automatically and blindly inherited from an earlier generation.

I offer you these words from the writings of the Bahá'í Faith. They are for Bahá'ís everywhere in the entire world, including Iran:

Beware! Beware! Lest ye offend any heart!
Beware! Beware! Lest ye hurt any soul!
Beware! Beware! Lest ye deal unkindly toward any person!
Beware! Beware! Lest ye be the cause of hopelessness to any creature!

Should a Bahá'í become the cause of grief to any human heart, or of despondency to any soul on earth, it were better for him or her to hide in the lowest depths of the earth than to walk upon the surface of the planet.

So much for Savak.

Mark the charge: Refuted!

5

Yazd

Some six hundred kilometres south of the capital of Iran is a city of nearly one hundred and fifty thousand inhabitants. It has a record of murder and savage persecution of Bahá'ís, extending over more than a hundred years. But there is something special about that record. Three times there have been 'seven martyrs of Yazd', in 1891, in 1955, and now again in 1980.

I shall always remember my own introduction to Yazd.

I was in Africa. It was the summer of 1955 when that first fateful cablegram reached me late in the day of July 28.

> FAMILY OF SEVEN, OLDEST EIGHTY AND
> YOUNGEST NINETEEN, WERE SET UPON BY
> MOB OF TWO THOUSAND STRONG, WHICH,
> ACCOMPANIED BY MUSIC OF DRUMS AND
> TRUMPETS, HACKED THEM TO PIECES WITH
> SPADES AND AXES.

This was the first time I had heard the name Yazd. I was to hear it many times, and to know it very well in the years ahead.

I left my work in Africa and came out to help defend my fellow Bahá'ís in Iran that summer. I was assisting in preparing a world-wide protest, a document called: *Bahá'í Appeal for Religious Freedom in Iran.*

Again it is summer. September 8, 1980.

Exactly a quarter of a century later!

Once more I am in Africa. There is another cablegram.
About Yazd!

SEVEN BAHÁ'IS, MEMBERS OF LOCAL SPIRI-
TUAL ASSEMBLY, TWO AUXILIARY BOARD
MEMBERS SHOT TO DEATH TODAY AT DAWN.

I came out of Africa the second time to help defend my
fellow Bahá'ís, who were once again being persecuted and
killed.

There was no need for my help this time. The Bahá'ís in
Iran were being ably and eloquently defended by the
institutions of the Bahá'í Faith in every part of the world,
and especially by the Bahá'í International Community at
the United Nations.

This left me free to launch my own one-man campaign,
my *Cry from the Heart*. Unofficial, personal, also world-
wide.

I had visited the city of Yazd myself in July, 1970. It
was the fifteenth anniversary of the month in which they
had so brutally slaughtered seven of my Bahá'í friends. I
wanted to see with my own eyes the scenes of their
heroism.

As I walked those quiet streets in Yazd, I had to keep
telling myself: 'It didn't happen in an arena in ancient
Rome. My friends were not slaughtered in medieval
Europe. They were killed right here. Only fifteen years
ago. Right here, only a few miles from where I am
standing now.' (See p. 42.)

Could it all have happened only fifteen years ago?

I soon *knew* that it could indeed.

Within an hour of my arrival, the Bahá'ís were
informed by the police that unless I left the city
immediately, there would be very severe consequences for
them. Especially for the members of their Local Spiritual
Assembly.

I knew only too well what those consequences might
be. Twice before the entire Local Spiritual Assembly had

been imprisoned. Once for three long years. One member
had died in that prison. I knew the consequences could be
far worse than imprisonment.

I returned from the Bahá'í Centre to my hotel, and
made plans to leave the city early the next morning. At
dawn I was ready to leave, but not before my dear Bahá'í
friends had made it possible for me to see the sites of those
past atrocities.

I stood in a small garden-like square, charmed by the
birds singing in the nearby trees. I wondered if the famous
bulbul, the Persian nightingale, sang its song of love and
beauty here in the late evening. I photographed the
archway leading to the site where once the enemies had
gathered to decide the fate of those Bahá'ís who
stubbornly refused to recant their Faith.

In case you still think I am exaggerating, come back
with me nearly a hundred years. We shall not make these
journeys back into Bahá'í history often, but in the case of
Yazd, it will help us to understand the present terrors in
Iran.

Close your eyes. You are with me here on the streets of
Yazd. It is May 19, 1891. Together we are moving quietly
among the crowd, watching our fellow Bahá'ís who have
been arrested and condemned to death.

Because they refuse to say, 'I am *not* a Bahá'í.'

It's all part of the game.

There are seven victims.

Naturally, it is Yazd.

May 19, 1891, was a day of great rejoicing for the
enemies of the Bahá'í Faith in Yazd. Dancers and
musicians with their trumpets, drums and tambourines
attended the party in numbers. They joyfully played and
danced around the seven victims as those poor souls were
herded from site to site along their scene of martyrdom on
the streets.

The tragedy began when Jalalu'd-Dawlih, the Prince-
Governor, returned in a happy frame of mind from his

hunt. The Prince invited the seven Bahá'ís who were the intended victims to what he called a friendly little intimate gathering. Before their arrival, he arranged for members of the clergy to hide behind a curtain. The Prince sought their help in condemning the Bahá'ís to death. He wanted to share the responsibility – just in case.

It would be so much more satisfying and pleasing if he could trap them into saying they were Bahá'ís – condemning themselves from their own lips.

How delicious!

Since they refused to say they were *not* followers of this religion, let them say they *were*, and die for it. This idea pleased him very much.

He pretended to befriend the seven victims. He feigned a very sympathetic manner.

'I am eager to know all about your Faith,' he told them. 'Prove to me that it is true. I may adopt it.'

The victims were silent at first. They suspected what was in his heart.

The Prince reassured them. 'You can safely speak out here. We are alone. No one will hear you but God and your Prince.'

The seven victims were aware of his evil purpose; they were not at all deceived by his ready smile. Still, they were always willing to offer proof of the truth of their Faith. Who knew what miracle might happen?

The Prince was delighted. He encouraged each one of them to confess, individually. Their words, with the clergy listening behind the curtain, were a certain death-warrant. There need be no delays in the public executions.

The Prince gave each one of the seven a gold coin as a reward, and dismissed them with a wave of his hand. The gold coins were taken away from them as soon as they left the room. They were seized, imprisoned, and prepared for death.

The Prince was delighted with the success of his stratagem.

The priests came out from behind the curtain at his bidding and eagerly and enthusiastically signed and sealed the death-warrants. They praised the Prince for his clever ruse, and congratulated each other. The fun was about to begin.

Nothing was more appreciated in Yazd than a first-class Bahá'í festival of death.

Early on the morning of May 19, 1891, by order of the Prince, trumpets, drums and tambourines were sounded to call the people together so that the merriment could begin. The prisoners whom the Prince had entrapped by his lies were already standing before him. He was willing, he said, to extend his mercy to the victims.

'You are young,' he said to the most youthful, who was twenty-seven. 'Do not be foolish. Recant your faith. Otherwise I shall be obliged to kill you.'

The young man replied coolly, 'I have offered my life in the path of God. Whoever wants it, let him come and take it.'

The Prince was angered by the answer. Immediately he called for a rope. He personally put it around the young man's neck. The executioner pulled on one end and the servants of the Prince jerked on the other. The boy was strangled to death amidst the applause of the onlookers. It was a mild beginning, but there were still six victims to go. From the site of that first martyrdom, the parade of death began.

Each place on the streets of Yazd where the victims were halted became honoured as the site of another slaughter. One of the seven was chosen to die at each separate site.

The crowd became infuriated when the prisoners would not beg for mercy or display fear. Especially when they contemptuously refused the demands of the mob to recant and curse their Faith.

Instead, the victims competed with each other for the honour of being the first to die. The anger and frustration of the mob turned into shrill cries of delight and pleasure as they beheld the second of the victims struck down before them.

This was more like it!

Slowly the parade went on to the next site. Another victim provided the entertainment. Yazd was not to be denied the full pleasure of its ghastly festival.

The mob refused to be satisfied. They hated the serenity of the victims, who continued to show no sign of fright, but instead fearlessly spoke to the crowd. They shared with them words from the teachings of their Faith. They offered forgiveness to their persecutors for all their cruel acts.

This only intensified the hatred and fury of the crowd. The mob began to cry out for more barbarous methods of killing the victims. Something hideous enough to terrify them.

A Dutch merchant, an eyewitness of this 1891 atrocity, reported via the Dutch Chargé d'Affaires, that the seven 'were executed quite unexpectedly. One was hung [strangled] in the presence of the Prince and six others were killed in different quarters of the town.' This eyewitness reported that all seven 'died like real martyrs without any fear and without saying anything but good about their religion.'

The mob insulted the remains of each fallen victim after his death in such a vicious and horrifying manner as could only degrade themselves and their city of Yazd.

Another account of these atrocities, by Captain Vaughan of the 7th Bengal Infantry, who passed through Yazd shortly after the event, points out that the martyrs' 'mangled remains were cut in pieces and exhibited to the victims' wives and children. I heard that the men who suffered showed great fortitude, and, though told that they had only to say . . . that their prophet was false, and their lives would be spared, scorned to do so.'

The crowds resorted to such gruesome and inhuman ways of trying to force words of fear and recantation from their victims, that I cannot bear to describe them for you. They are available for you to read if you have the heart.* I cannot bear to write about them here on these pages, they are so horrendous.

All seven heroic victims were finally slain on that long-ago day in 1891, and at last, the merry-making ended. The music stopped; the dancing ceased. The festival of death was over!

There were no more victims.

It had been quite a day.

Even for Yazd.

The remains of the seven martyrs were thrown into a pit in the desert on the edge of the city. A favourite burying-place for Bahá'ís.

A holiday was declared by the Governor, the Prince, whose treachery had started it all. Shops were closed by his order.

'It is a time for rejoicing, not business,' he announced.

The sun eventually went down on May 19, 1891.

On Tuesday morning, the Prince ordered that the illumination of the city, planned for Tuesday night, should be stopped, and warned that anyone who mentioned the killing of the seven would have his tongue cut out.

The world was becoming aware of the terrible thing that had happened in Yazd, and a curtain of silence was being drawn over the whole episode. Too late.

The British Chargé d'Affaires told the Shah that he would 'deeply regret if, at any time, anything should be

---

* See *God Passes By*, by Shoghi Effendi, pp. 201–2 (Bahá'í Publishing Trust, Wilmette, Illinois, 1970); and *The Bábí and Bahá'í Religions, 1844–1944*, ed. by Moojan Momen, chap. 20.

done which may injure the reputation of the Persian Government.'

Yazd was a specialist in doing just that.

These events of May 19, 1891 have been described as 'one of the most barbarous acts ever perpetrated in modern times.'

You can open your eyes now.

It is time for us to go home as well, and leave Yazd. We no longer need dwell on either May 19, 1891, or July 28, 1955.

We can forget the past, for it has happened all over again.

Now. In our time. September 8, 1980!

Can you believe it? Same city, Yazd. Same crime. Same number of martyrs – seven.

Once again I am in Africa. I am holding in my hand another cablegram. About Yazd.

This time it is a headline taken from the Yazd Television announcement:

> SEPTEMBER 8, 1980. YAZD, IRAN – SEVEN
> BAHA'I SPIES SHOT TO DEATH TODAY AT
> DAWN.

Among the *Seven Martyrs of Yazd,* September 8, 1980, was 'Azízu'lláh D̲h̲abíḥíyán.

He was a member of the Bahá'í Auxiliary Board. He was arrested in Shiraz, that city where the Bahá'í Faith was born, and where the friends had already suffered severely from the current persecutions. Members of the Local Spiritual Assembly of Shiraz and members of the Auxiliary Board had been arrested, summarily tried, and executed. 'Azízu'lláh D̲h̲abíḥíyán had gone to Shiraz to console and comfort the survivors.

I was an Auxiliary Board member myself for many years, and although I may not have been the greatest, I *do* know that an Auxiliary Board member's whole life is consecrated to visiting the Bahá'ís, to encouraging them, and helping them to live better lives of service to all men, and to become more useful members of their own communities, examples for friends and neighbours alike.

Today in Iran they are being hunted down, like 'Azízu'lláh Dhabíhíyán in Shiraz, and they are being killed. As they killed him.

'Azízu'lláh Dhabíhíyán, my friend, was fifty-six. He was one of the seven to die at dawn in that small garden outside Yazd. He was tied to a tree with his six companions and shot to death.

'Azízu'lláh was quite accustomed to being tied to a tree and shot at. His captors in Shiraz gave him many rehearsals for death on the way back to Yazd. They would stop the car frequently and amidst much ribald laughter, they would pull 'Azízu'lláh roughly out of the car, push him toward a nearby tree and tie him to it. They told 'Azízu'lláh that it was too much trouble to take him all the way back to Yazd. They were going to execute him now. Right here.

'Azízu'lláh could, of course, prevent his death by denying that he was a Bahá'í. He could beg for mercy. They always gave the Bahá'ís that choice. Otherwise, they said, 'Azízu'lláh would die immediately.

When 'Azízu'lláh refused, they fired their guns at his head, deliberately missing. Several times on the way they repeated their little game, and their fake execution, telling 'Azízu'lláh that this time it was for real. Still they could not make him waver or recant.

Their abuse became more violent and spiteful each time they failed. They continued to fire the bullets around his body, coming as close as possible.

They tired of their sport, threw 'Azízu'lláh into the car, and drove him directly to the death-prison of Yazd where he joined his companions.

The next time 'Azízu'lláh Dhabíhíyán would be tied to a tree, it would be at dawn. In Yazd. He would be shot to death with his six Bahá'í companions, each one of whom had displayed the same heroism and courage.

I would like you to meet one of these fearsome criminals, these spies for Israel. His name is 'Abdu'l-Vahháb Kázimí. He is from Manshad village quite near to Yazd.

He is so old, that his age was estimated between eighty-five and ninety. So stooped was he, that when he walked, his fingers almost touched the ground.

Everyone could see what a 'threat to the nation' this 'spy for Israel' was!

When on the morning of September 8, 1980, it was rumoured that *six* Bahá'ís were to be shot to death, the rumour was immediately denounced by the Bahá'ís as a lie.

'It is never *six* Bahá'ís that die in YAZD. It is *seven,* or none!'

'Abdu'l-Vahháb Kázimí Manshádí was on his way to Yazd under arrest. He didn't know it, but he was to be the *seventh.*

He hadn't made it easy for the authorities. They would be glad when they were done with this frail but fierce old man. He knew the words of the Koran so well, that he was known as a 'walking Koran', and corrected his persecutors at the trial when they made a wrong quotation from that Holy Book to try and prove the faithlessness of the Bahá'í prisoners to Islam.

A few months before, his home in Manshad had been raided. Naturally, he was a Bahá'í. It was expected in such times of trouble. His Bahá'í books were confiscated. His storeroom was set on fire. His only recourse was prayer. They interrupted his prayers by kicking him to the ground, and beating him so badly that his wife, who witnessed this bestial assault, died of shock a few days later.

Everyone knew there was worse to come. It was beginning to happen everywhere. His friends and family entreated the old man to leave Manshad at once for his own safety. He refused.

'I will not leave my trench,' he said. 'I will stay and defend it.'

A second time they raided 'Abdu'l-Vahháb's home. This time, after beating him, they threw him into the official car that was to bring him to Yazd. But he was so old and crippled, and wounded from his beatings, that it hardly seemed worth the efforts of the Revolutionary Guards to carry him all the way to Yazd. They debated whether they should toss him into the road, run the car over him a few times, and have done with it.

Instead, they decided to push the old man out of the car into the midst of the desert. It was night-time, and they were confident that with his wounds and his weak state he would surely perish.

'Too much time is being wasted on one old man,' they declared.

He was *not* just one old man. He was the *seventh*.

'Abdu'l-Vahháb was an old man with a defiant spirit. He refused to die just for the convenience of the Revolutionary Guards. Slowly and painfully he raised himself up and set out for home. A passing car took pity on his bent figure and brought him back to a village fourteen kilometres from Manshad. Through the hills and the desert, on foot, the old man painfully took the short cut home.

When he was seen there the next day, alive, and working about his home, the bullies were outraged. What did they have to do to kill one weak old man?

They seized him again. This time, they said, they would end it. They took him directly to Yazd and threw him into prison.

When 'Abdu'l-Vahháb's friends heard that he was condemned to death, they shook their heads in wonder.

'How,' they said, 'will they shoot this poor old man?'
'He is too bent over to be executed by a firing-squad.'

They were wrong.

They shot the old man three times in the abdomen. When he fell, they shot him in the head.

His crime: He was a Bahá'í.

Thus, 'Abdu'l-Vahháb Kázimí Man<u>sh</u>ádí joined his six fellow Bahá'ís and became the seventh martyr.

He died at dawn with the others.

The old man was in love with all the Messengers of God, and all the holy Books. Especially did he love the eloquent words of Muhammad whom he was falsely accused of betraying.

6

The House of the Báb

The beautiful room you will see on the next page was the site where the Bahá'í Faith was born. From that single lamp, the Light of the Faith of the Báb and Bahá'u'lláh has covered the face of the earth; from one believer in that room, on that historic night in 1844, there are now Bahá'ís in more than one hundred thousand centres in almost every part of the planet.

That room was in the House of the Báb in the heart of the city of Shiraz, a city which, in the last four years, has suffered a storm of terror, destruction and murder.

A single lamp marked the spot where the Báb sat when He spoke those first soul-stirring, electrifying words to Mullá Ḥusayn, the first to believe in Him, on that long-ago wondrous night. The Báb declared that it was the dawn of a New Day in the fortunes of mankind. He was the Herald of an even greater Figure yet to come. He *was* the Dawn, the One to follow soon after Him would be the Sun.

They were to usher in that wondrous Day of God foretold in all the Holy Scriptures, a time of peace, prosperity and happiness for all mankind.

The room is gone now. The House is gone. The outward body has been destroyed. But the inward soul of that much-loved structure lives on today in the hearts of millions of Bahá'ís. Millions more tomorrow.

I sat in that room, and read from *The Dawn-Breakers,*

Upper chamber of the House of the Báb in Shíráz where
He announced His Mission to Mullá Ḥusayn

an historical account of that moment, on that night so long ago.

The words of Mullá Ḥusayn were as fresh as on the day he wrote them.

> This Revelation, so suddenly and impetuously thrust upon me, came as a thunderbolt which, for a time, seemed to have benumbed my faculties. I was blinded by its dazzling splendour and overwhelmed by its crushing force. Excitement, joy, awe, and wonder stirred the depths of my soul. Predominant among these emotions was a sense of gladness and strength which seemed to have transfigured me. How feeble and impotent, how dejected and timid, I had felt previously! ... Now, however, the knowledge of His Revelation had galvanized my being. I felt possessed of such courage and power that were the world, all its peoples and its potentates, to rise against me, I would, alone and undaunted, withstand their onslaught ... I seemed to be the Voice of Gabriel personified, calling unto all mankind: 'Awake, for, lo! the morning Light has broken. Arise, for His Cause is made manifest. The portal of His grace is open wide; enter therein, O peoples of the world! For He Who is your promised One is come!'*

With closed eyes as I sat there across from that lamp, that scene of inexpressible splendour was unveiled before me. Like Mullá Ḥusayn, I, too, nearly one hundred and forty years later, was enraptured by that unique experience. Like Mullá Ḥusayn, I, too, was lost in the wonder and joy of my successful quest for my Beloved.

I had found the Báb and Bahá'u'lláh in far-off Salt Lake City, Utah, in North America. Yet here I was in Shiraz!

Hearts, from the two polar seas, from the Mediterra-

* From Nabíl-i-A'ẓam, *The Dawn-Breakers* (Bahá'í Publishing Trust, Wilmette, Illinois, 1932), p. 65.

nean, and the Atlantic, Pacific, and Indian Oceans, have been drawn, as Mullá Ḥusayn was drawn, to that Holy House, as steel-filings are drawn to a magnet.

That Holy House belonged to mankind, not Iran.

Perhaps now it is easier to understand why one of the most poignant and saddest news stories for the Bahá'ís of the world was the report of the desecration and destruction of this precious House of the Báb. The tragic news reached them that this holy place of pilgrimage had first been vandalized, then torn down, and finally completely levelled to the ground. The ruins were eventually swept away by a bulldozer.

The news rejoiced the religious authorities in Iran as much as it saddened the Bahá'ís. The Báb Himself had suffered at the hands of the clergy and people of this city. His followers had been persecuted here from the earliest days. In like manner, this noble House more than once had, in its turn, been forced to bear the wounds of the destroyers. On the first occasion, 1942–43, it was attacked and a fire was started, after which it was restored to its original design. The second time was in 1955 during the reign of Muhammad Reza Shah, whom the Bahá'ís are accused of supporting, when it was vandalized and looted, its walls, doors and windows reduced to rubble. It was again restored.

'Uncontrollable mobs' were blamed then for demolishing this structure. Those same false statements have been repeated again by the present regime in Iran, during the current wave of persecutions in Shiraz.

Crowds of people over whom they had no control, the authorities said, were responsible for assaulting the House of the Báb. The authorities themselves, of course, were blameless.

Eyewitnesses have told quite a different story. For three days they watched the mobs, instigated and encouraged by the fanatical clergy of Shiraz, pursue their vicious attack on this Bahá'í Holy Place.

There are motion pictures to verify this fact.

Soon looters had stripped that Holy House to a bare skeleton. The room where the Báb met Mullá Ḥusayn was totally dismantled. The doors and windows of the lower story were removed. The entire structure was defaced.

At that point the destruction stopped temporarily. The Government stepped in and announced that Bahá'í properties throughout the entire country had been seized by the authorities in order to protect them. This protection included all Bahá'í Holy Places.

It soon became clear that the Báb's House had been seized, *not* to protect it, as the authorities had announced, but that the old secret plan to destroy the House completely, step by step, might go forward unhindered.

What is, and will, in time, be recognized to be one of the holiest sites in the religious history of mankind, fell into the demonic grasp of the mullas of Shiraz, and was, for the time being, doomed.

There is on file with the Bahá'ís an Order from the Revolutionary Guards of the Province of Fars, of which Shiraz is the capital, dated April 13, 1979, and presented to the Custodian of the House of the Báb. This Order *certifies* that the holy House of the Báb had been seized and occupied 'In Trust' by the Government so they might protect it from being destroyed.

It turned out to be entrusting the *sheep* to the *wolf.*

The authorities knew from the beginning what the plan was. The depths of their debasement and complete lack of integrity were further demonstrated when it was learned that plans had been developing long before the destruction took place, in order to give them time to raise enough money not only to destroy the House, but to obliterate the site.

They planned, even at that early date, to build roads and a square which would ultimately erase all signs of what had once stood on that sacred spot.

All this was conceived and organized long before the

Destruction of the House of the Báb,
Shiraz, 1979

'unruly' mobs and 'uncontrollable' crowds under the careful direction of the clergy, and on their behalf, took the first threatening and deadly steps against that much-loved holy Place.

The sum of one hundred million tumans* was allocated for the project. There were dissenting voices. The Mayor and the Chief of the Central Economic Council of Teheran both said that money should be spent to *build* and not to *demolish.*

Both these men were dismissed from their jobs and transferred. Their replacements were chosen for their antagonism to the Bahá'í Faith. They were thus ideally suited to this work of betraying promises and breaking oaths.

Forty million tumans were approved almost at the start. The Governor of Shiraz also offered a share of the budget.

Please note: They received no money from the 'unruly' mobs and 'uncontrollable' crowds.

Their written oath that they had seized the Báb's Holy House to hold it 'in trust' has been broken.

It is often necessary, they said, to take devious actions against such people as the Bahá'ís who are enemies of Islam. So they broke their 'oath' and betrayed their 'trust'.

Apparently not one of these noble supporters of Islam in the Islamic Revolution can read Arabic.

No one in this regime, either religious or civil, a regime led by a clergy that boasts its knowledge of thousands and thousands of memorized passages from the Koran and the sacred traditions, was apparently even the least bit familiar with the words of their own Prophet, Muhammad: from the Koran.

The Bahá'ís know them, and keep them.

Not, however, the present regime in Iran.

Muhammad says plainly:

* about ten million dollars

Fulfil the covenant of God when ye have entered into it, and break not your oaths after ye have confirmed them. Indeed ye have made God your surety; for God knoweth all ye do. (Koran 16:93)

Ask yourself, which is the friend? And which the enemy of Islam? In Shiraz.

The Orange Tree

The Bahá'ís of Iran, indignant at this senseless destruction of a Holy Place belonging to the largest religious minority in the land, sent telegrams and letters of protest to the Head of the Government.

These messages were of no avail.

The Bahá'í World Community made an even more urgent appeal.

Its cablegrams were likewise ignored.

The clergy had launched their plan of death for this Holy House; they would allow nothing to interfere with their obliteration of it. If they could not successfully exterminate the entire Bahá'í community in Iran, as rapidly as they wished, they could at least totally remove all trace of that hated place where the Bahá'í Faith had been born.

As a special insult, they cut down the orange tree which the Báb had planted with His own hands in the courtyard of that lovely House. They sliced the tree trunk in two, burned both halves, and threw the remnants in the trash.

Many Bahá'í pilgrims have eaten fruit from that orange tree. When they made their pilgrimage to that holy House, they would take tea in the garden. Now, the enemies had gone out of their way to destroy spitefully and maliciously that symbol of love and fellowship. I myself have sat in that lovely, cool, tree-shaded garden, and enjoyed hearing stories about the Báb and His family from the caretaker, a descendant of the Báb.

I also had tea, and an orange from that tree. One of my

The orange tree planted by the Báb in the courtyard of His
House in Shiraz

sweetest memories of Iran is to recall those happy hours spent in the House of the Báb on my two separate visits to Shiraz.

Now there is nothing but an empty space.

Still, I can see the House as clearly as ever. It will always be like that with every Bahá'í who has been blessed by visiting that wondrous Site.

I can't help but wonder at the foolishness of such enemies. Don't they know that they really haven't cut down that orange tree at all?

I, personally, have at least seven friends in North America who right now are eating oranges from the trees they have grown from the seeds of that orange tree planted by the Báb in Shiraz. There are hundreds more. Pilgrims from everywhere have taken home oranges and planted seeds from that tree.

Don't the authorities in Iran know that *tomorrow,* if access to Iran were permitted, black, yellow, red, brown and white Bahá'ís could fly in from all over the world, and plant *a whole row* of orange trees all round the city of Shiraz? From the trees grown from the seeds of the tree they *thought* they had cut down.

That is the real symbol.

Everything which the present regime in Iran thinks they have destroyed is alive! It thrives and prospers on their savage brutality. Don't they realize yet that, in the end, they will be completely frustrated and defeated?

Don't they know that because of these wicked and senseless actions, right now, the world over, thousands of additional orange trees are being planted from the drying seeds of that 'House-of-the-Báb' orange tree?

The increased and carefully nurtured planting began the moment the news of the destruction of that orange tree was received.

The battle is on!

Each Bahá'í orange tree in every part of the world, fully grown and tender shoot alike, is waiting to have the honour of being the first to replace the orange tree those foolish enemies thought they had cut down.

And that day will surely come.

Whatever the enemies of the Bahá'í Faith do, in any part of that land of Iran, to attack and obliterate God's new Message, is ultimately fruitless. *They* are transient, the Faith of the Báb and Bahá'u'lláh is eternal. Its roots are planted deep down in the friendly soil of human hearts the world over. The Bahá'í Faith is the Cause of God, not of man. Therein lies the difference.

The fanatical clergy in Iran have lost the beautiful spirit of Muhammad, and are rootless and lifeless in their graves of error, exactly as the Apostle of God Himself foretold they would be. They will eventually see the bankruptcy of all their nefarious schemes, and the poison of their own hatred will in the end consume them.

I didn't say that. Sacred Scriptures said it. Including their own.

It is a retelling in our day of the eternal story of the triumph which every world religion has won over its most bitter enemies.

It is always the *Cause of God* against the *cause of man.*

Therefore, the end is obvious.

Three times the enemies of the Bahá'í Faith have tried to destroy this Holy House of the Báb. Each time their attempts have been more violent and the results more devastating. Following each attempt, there has been a far greater number of new Bahá'ís in more and more countries of the world to protest. Now, the indignation is world-wide. Their crime has now become a world crime bringing shame to Shiraz from over one hundred thousand centres where their vandalism is deplored and denounced. Not only among Bahá'ís, among mankind.

This very international crime may be the one which in the end will bring about their downfall.

'The Hand of God is over the hand of man.'

The House of the Báb is gone.

A street and an open square now occupy the site where once stood that much-loved, sacred and beautiful House. The street is empty. But the breezes of God still blow across it, carrying its fragrance to the nostrils of His loved ones.

Don't they know that in the days to come, that beautiful House will stand once again exactly as it stood in the days when the blessed Báb walked the streets of His native city?

Don't they know that every stone, every door, every window, every single part of that precious Holy House is not only engraved forever in the minds of its lovers, but even more significantly, has been photographed both in black-and-white and in colour?

There are detailed architects' drawings, blue prints, floor plans and all the building and construction information necessary to restore that Holy House exactly as it was before.

This information is preserved and protected in several places around the planet.

It is safe from the hands of the enemy.

Twice already that House has been restored. It will be restored a third time.

When, is not important. The fact is inevitable.

This Holy House can never be destroyed, for the Hand of God is over the hand of man.

It will be a place of Pilgrimage in ages to come for millions of people.

That House will stand exactly as it was, exactly where it stood, in every detail, with all its simplicity and beauty.

'So it is written and so it shall be.'

Bahá'u'lláh Himself has addressed one of the Ministers of Nasiri'd-Din Shah, concerning their futile attempts to obliterate His Faith:

Dost thou believe thou hast the power to frustrate His Will, to hinder Him from executing His judgement, or to deter Him from exercising His sovereignty? Pretendest thou that aught in the heavens or in the earth can resist His Faith? No, by Him Who is the Eternal Truth! Nothing whatsoever in the whole of creation can thwart His Purpose.

The words which the Báb spoke on that historic night so long ago, in that Holy House on the eve of the birth of the Bahá'í Faith, attest the eternal truth of this statement.

This night, this very hour will, in the days to come, be celebrated as one of the greatest and most significant of all festivals.

It has been, and is, every year.

Those wondrous words heralding the coming of the 'Christ-promised Kingdom of God on Earth' will be spoken again in that same room, on that same Site, on that same day, and the enemies who tried to erase God's religion from the face of Shiraz will be forgotten and no man will remember them.

The children's-children of those 'unruly mobs' so deceitfully duped by the clergy, will join in those days their fellow Bahá'ís in pilgrimage to that Holy House, and no one will ever think that there was a time when they did not love each other.

That is the power of the love of God and His Messengers.

'So it is written, and so it shall be.'

7

Terrible Teheran

1

The newspaper *Kayhan* of Teheran, in one of its recent issues, told the world why the Bahá'ís were being killed. The reason?

*For the crime of treason to
the Muslim nation of Iran.*

It added that the Bahá'ís were not only a 'danger' to the nation, but to the Islamic Revolution, and to every Muslim in the country.

I want you to meet one of these 'dangerous' Bahá'í criminals who threaten the city of Teheran and its peoples. His name is Ḥakím. Professor Manúchihr Ḥakím. The people of Teheran, both Bahá'í and Muslim, and every other religion, know him best as 'Doctor Ḥakím'.

He was shot to death in his clinic on January 12, 1981.

A few months before his death, Dr Ḥakím was in Europe, in France, where he is honoured and revered. His family and friends warned him not to return to Iran.

'It is very dangerous for you.'

'You will be killed this time.'

But in spite of their warnings and entreaties, Dr Ḥakím would not listen.

'It is my duty to return to Teheran,' he said.

Not only because the Bahá'í community there needed

him in their time of terrible trouble, but because he was a doctor. All his patients needed him. Even those who were Muslim, Christian, Zoroastrian – whatever their religion. He was their doctor. They depended upon him. They trusted him. He must be faithful to that trust.

It was the Bahá'í way, stronger even than the Hippocratic oath. Besides, Teheran was his home town. He was born there. He loved Teheran.

'No,' Dr Ḥakím said, 'I must return to Teheran.' And he went back, despite his knowledge of the danger to his life.

One afternoon shortly after his return, he was closing his clinic. His last patient had left. It had been a long and busy day. There were many sick.

He was alone in the clinic.

Suddenly, unexpectedly, a different kind of patient entered: unidentified gunmen. They shot him to death and left. His nurse found him later, lying in a pool of blood.

The authorities made no effort whatsoever to identify or bring to justice his assailants. No one came forward to identify them. People had seen strangers leaving, but who they were, they could not or would not say.

The authorities disclaimed any responsibility. It was, they said, quite obviously the work of a terrorist group, undoubtedly one which was antagonistic to the Bahá'í Faith. Dr Ḥakím had unfortunately been caught in the web.

Antagonistic is a mild word for *shot down in cold blood.*

Dr Ḥakím had been the object of repeated threats against his life for some time. He ignored them and went on with his work. The authorities repeatedly denied that they were involved in any way with these threats, but it was the authorities who interrogated him, not some unknown terrorist group. He was ordered to surrender the list of the names of Bahá'í physicians throughout Iran.

He refused.

From that time on, until the day of his death, Dr Ḥakím received frequent anonymous threats against his life, and many obscene phone calls about his religion. The authorities knew it was hopeless to say to such a courageous and dedicated man:

'Recant your faith. Deny you are a Bahá'í, or we will kill you.'

Dr Ḥakím made it unmistakably clear to the authorities that on the subject of his belief in Bahá'u'lláh and in the Bahá'í Faith, he would stand as steadfast as the Alburz Mountains north of the city.

In replying to the complaints from the Bahá'í community concerning Dr Ḥakím's cruel and brutal assassination, the authorities in Teheran repeated their earlier denials. The murderer was completely unknown to them. They themselves were puzzled by this unexpected killing, they said. They disclaimed any involvement. They told the Bahá'ís that undoubtedly it was the work of *Fada'iyan-i-Islam*, the militant terrorist group already described.

However, a few days after the assassination, officials went to his house to make, they said, an official inventory. They sealed the house. The next day about twenty Revolutionary Guards entered and removed everything. They took Dr Ḥakím's car from the garage, and left the house and premises stripped bare.

The Bahá'í Hospital in Teheran, which Dr Ḥakím had helped to establish, had, some months before, been occupied. All Bahá'í personnel were dismissed. Documents, records, personal papers were confiscated. Even the old people were evicted from the Home for the Aged associated with the hospital. They had no place to go. Many of them had no families. No money. Nothing.

The authorities had already confiscated the Bahá'í Company that took care of their small pensions and supported them. When the old people lost Dr Ḥakím, they lost all, including a loving father and a kind son.

The most 'antagonistic' group of 'terrorists', up to this

point in our story, has always been those authorized by the present regime; so there was little hope that the criminals who had committed this foul crime against a much-loved doctor would ever be apprehended.

Their plans for the elimination of the Bahá'í community in Iran had taken an important step forward. Another prominent Bahá'í had been struck down. Others would soon follow.

The pattern of death in Iran is clear. Those who are executed have their properties confiscated.

Dr Ḥakím who was perhaps too popular to be 'tried' was, instead, assassinated. The fact that a few days after his murder his house and belongings were totally confiscated, shows all too clearly, in spite of their denials, the complicity of those in authority.

Dr Manúchihr Ḥakím, humanitarian, loved by thousands, Bahá'ís and non-Bahá'ís alike, was on their death-list.

2

Yes, I knew him. Very well indeed. He was one of my doctors during my visits to Iran. I met him first in the very clinic where they shot him down. I can see his office quite plainly. I can look down and visualize the spot where he lay, a sacrifice to his humanitarian services.

And that is not *my* assessment of him; it is the consensus of his peers, the doctors the world over who knew, loved and respected him.

I met Dr Manúchihr Ḥakím later when I was treated in the Bahá'í Hospital which he had helped found. The nurses and patients said it was like sunshine coming into their rooms when Dr Ḥakím entered. He made each patient feel that he or she was the only patient under his care.

I know.

He made me feel that way.

86   A CRY FROM THE HEART

It is very easy for me to tell you about this man, so 'dangerous' to the city of Teheran and its people. Nothing could give me more pleasure.

Dr Manúchihr Ḥakím was a native of Teheran. Born there. Died there. One of the great ones. Even his enemies, in the days to come, will honour his name. Many in Iran do already. Cautiously.

Dr Ḥakím was born in 1911, the son of a notable physician, and thus had a splendid start upon his illustrious medical career. He took his degree at the Medical College in Paris, then won the *agrégation* for professorial rank in the Universities of France. He was renowned for his researches in anatomy, his discoveries being twice cited in *Le Rouvier*, the standard work on anatomy. His writings have become part of the textbooks used in many medical colleges.

Dr Manúchihr Ḥakím returned to Iran in 1938 where he established a Chair of Anatomy at the University of Teheran. His books are still being used as texts in that field.

He was also a well-known specialist in gastroenterology.

Dr Ḥakím was Director of the Bahá'í Hospital in Teheran ever since its inception. He served in this capacity for thirty years. He also founded the Bahá'í Home for the Aged, associated with the hospital. This home accepted people of all religious and racial backgrounds.

Dr Ḥakím was decorated by the French Government with the Légion d'honneur in 1976 for his humanitarian services to mankind.

Ask yourself, *Who was the loser?*

The authorities in Iran made it evident that they were pleased by his death, but what about the poor and the sick from among their own people? What about the suffering who had received help, comfort, kindness and generosity from this great man? Many of these so-called 'enemies'

Dr Manúc̲h̲ihr Ḥakím, assassinated in Teheran,
January 12, 1981

cried when they heard the sad news of his death. They sent messages of condolence. They loved Dr Ḥakím.

The Government of France had decorated him because he was a humanitarian. The authorities in Iran killed him because he was a Bahá'í.

For over a quarter of a century, Dr Manúchihr Ḥakím was a member, and several times Chairman, of the National Spiritual Assembly of the Bahá'ís of Iran.

That is why he was killed.

When the news of his murder was flashed around the world, bringing Teheran into the murder spotlight yet another time, one of the television commentators described that capital city as 'Terroran'.

He was right.

3

The Bahá'ís of Teheran were determined to show the regime in Iran, and the whole world, what they thought of this great human being, Dr Manúchihr Ḥakím.

The authorities warned the Baha'ís not to make a big public display of their feelings on the occasion of his funeral. The smaller the funeral, they said, the better it would be for all concerned. Especially the Bahá'ís.

It should be taken as a threat.

The number of Bahá'ís who had earlier turned out in defiance of the present regime to demonstrate their love for the fallen victims in Shiraz, Tabriz, and Yazd had caused considerable worry and annoyance to the authorities. The Bahá'í participation was always orderly, peaceful and non-violent, but they refused to let their heroes go to their graves without a proper tribute to their honour, their courage, and their greatness.

The authorities didn't want these expressions of love repeated in Teheran on a larger scale. *They* would provide the escort for the body, they said. All the way. There had better be no trouble. They made it very clear to the

Bahá'ís that it might become extremely dangerous for those who dared to participate this time. The Bahá'ís would regret any foolish actions. Or there might be additional funerals for the Bahá'í community to worry about.

This, however, was Dr Manúchihr Ḥakím they were talking about, and the Bahá'ís were determined to honour his life of service. What happened to any of them was of little consequence. They would show their respect for this great man, this wonderful servant of the Bahá'í Faith, come what may. The authorities could do as they pleased. If necessary, they were prepared to die *en masse* on the way to that hero's grave.

It all began quite quietly.

A few courageous and devoted Bahá'í youth went to the Coroner's office to claim the body of their dear friend and father. They had been told to be very wise and very careful. Brave they were already.

The Local Spiritual Assembly of Teheran was in charge of the funeral. They had planned it carefully and beautifully, so that it might live up to the spirit of the Bahá'í teachings on death.

Bahá'u'lláh had written:

I have made death a messenger of joy to thee.
Wherefore dost thou grieve?

Death is not the ending, but the beginning of life. The perfume bottle is broken, and the fragrance gone somewhere else.

The Bahá'ís knew that wherever Dr Ḥakím had gone, he had been welcomed with open arms. His fellow Bahá'ís were determined that he should have a beautiful and joyous send-off from this world which he had served so long and so faithfully.

His body was transported to the cemetery in an ambulance. No one had ever seen an ambulance like that ambulance before. It was literally covered with flowers

from one end to the other. There were floral wreaths of
every shape and colour. A coat of glory and beauty for Dr
Ḥakím's final journey.

The flowers were not anonymous. Every Bahá'í Local
Spiritual Assembly in Iran wished to be identified with
the good doctor. It did not matter what the authorities
might say or do, or how upset they might be by this show
of solidarity. This was Dr Ḥakím's hour and no one could
take it from him.

Cablegrams of praise and sympathy were pouring in
from all parts of the world.

Anyone standing on the streets of Teheran could
plainly read the names printed on those magnificent
wreaths of beautiful flowers. They came from every city
where his fellow Bahá'ís had been shot to death, from the
relatives of those already fallen companions who would
be waiting to greet and congratulate him on his own
marvellous ending.

It was a proud company in which Dr Ḥakím was
making his last journey through the streets of his native
city.

The floral wreaths cried out their message of love and
defiance:

> *The National Spiritual Assembly of the Bahá'ís of Iran*
> (his Assembly for so many years)

> *The Local Spiritual Assembly of Shiraz* (where the Báb
> had been born)

> *The Local Spiritual Assembly of Tabriz* (where He had
> been martyred)

> *The Local Spiritual Assembly of Teheran* (where
> Bahá'u'lláh had been born, stoned, and imprisoned)

The floral wreaths by their very names told the story of
the suffering of the entire Bahá'í community in Iran.
They all showed their love and disregard of danger:

Yazd	*Hamadan*	*Abadan*
Mashhad	*Abidih*	*Kirman*
Isfahan	*Kirmanshah*	*Karaj*

On and on they went. Some fifty Bahá'í centres were represented on that flower-laden ambulance as it made its fragrant way slowly through the city of Teheran toward the cemetery.

Bahá'ís had not gathered in large numbers at the starting-place. Instead, they joined the procession a few at a time as it made its journey toward its final destination.

Revolutionary Guards, guns at the ready, walked beside the ambulance all the way, guarding it, watching the streets. They were prepared for any trouble that might come. Any unexpected violent demonstration by the Bahá'ís of Teheran would be dealt with. Wherever so many people gather it means trouble, the Revolutionary Guards believed.

They never learn about the Bahá'ís, do they?

The only demonstration was one of love. Lips moving in silent prayer. But it was overwhelming. When that garden of flowers, the ambulance, finally arrived at the cemetery, there were *four thousand* Bahá'ís in attendance.

The Local Spiritual Assembly of Teheran had arranged for beautiful prayers and readings to be heard through the loudspeakers. The speakers had been installed in the most lovely surroundings of the Teheran cemetery. The area was thronged with Bahá'í faces.

Radiant. Proud. Unafraid.

Every Bahá'í had been thrilled and inspired by seeing the National Spiritual Assembly members leading the procession, and the Local Spiritual Assembly of Teheran in line behind them, all disregarding their own personal safety, unafraid of any dire consequences which might follow.

That courageous demonstration had a great impact on every Bahá'í present. They all arose spontaneously to follow that brave leadership.

The Funeral of Dr Manúchihr Ḥakím

In the middle of the ceremony, an urgent telephone call came from the Security Office. The Bahá'ís were informed that at the cemetery three bombs had been planted in the area! If the cemetery were not evacuated immediately, the authorities said, they would not be responsible for the consequences. Masses could be killed. It would be better, they insisted, if the Bahá'ís would immediately disperse and leave the cemetery. The funeral of Dr Ḥakím could go on very well without them. The cemetery authorities would see that he was buried.

This information was broadcast over the loudspeakers. It was received in stony silence.

No Bahá'í moved.

Instead, the funeral ceremony of Dr Ḥakím continued serenely as though it had never been interrupted, and no announcement and threat ever made.

After the closing prayer, when the body of Dr Ḥakím was being carried to its final resting-place, the Bahá'ís began to chant more prayers. In unison. A few at first. Softly, then slowly growing in volume. Soon the entire four thousand had joined in. It sounded as though they were storming the gates of heaven for Dr Ḥakím.

They made the countryside echo with the majesty of their prayer. It seemed as though they were sounding the call as far as Tabriz and Yazd and Shiraz where their other loved ones had fallen, in order to comfort the relatives of those dear souls too.

People some distance from the entrance to the cemetery turned around to listen.

As the Bahá'ís walked toward the vault where Dr Ḥakím's remains would be placed, they chanted the battle cry which had been raised by the heroes of Fort Ṭabarsí.* The words called upon God to help and fortify them and strengthen their hearts against the enemy. Like the battle-

* The scene of an heroic episode during the ministry of the Báb (1844–50).

cry 'Yá Ṣáḥibu'z-Zamán!' – 'O Lord of the Age!' – in praise of the Báb, their chant rang out with fervour and devotion, thrilling every heart.

Before they left their dear friend for the last time, that huge crowd once more began chanting in unison. It was a prayer for the protection of the entire Bahá'í community of Iran. It was a prayer given to them by the Báb for just such times of difficulties and distress as they were now facing everywhere in that unhappy land.

Is there any Remover of difficulties save God? Say: Praised be God! He is God! All are His servants and all abide by His bidding!

Bahá'ís the world over were praying with them on that day. Many were undoubtedly reciting that very same prayer, unaware of the thrilling things that were happening in that far-off cemetery.

One would have thought by looking at those Bahá'ís with their radiant smiles, their closed ranks of unity, that they had been on a picnic, a time of joy and happiness. And in a way, it had been. They had fulfilled Bahá'u'lláh's words to the very end: 'I have made death a messenger of joy to thee. Wherefore dost thou grieve?'

Most important of all, Dr Manúchihr Ḥakím had been given one of the greatest gifts of all, a 'good ending': both as a martyr for his Faith and with a loving farewell from his friends everywhere.

As I read those reports from Teheran about that dramatic occasion with its ambulance, flowers, marching Bahá'ís, threat of bombs, their serene indifference to danger, the chorus of four thousand voices chanting together, it was hard to believe that it was a reality, and not a fantasy. It was like watching a motion picture, a cloak-and-dagger adventure story, with a tremendous victorious finish with virtue and God triumphant. I remembered my own visit to that Teheran cemetery to pay tribute to the early heroes of the Faith. I thought to myself:

'Wouldn't it be wonderful, if we could all be present at a confrontation in the next world between Dr Ḥakím and the authorities who ordered his death? Imagine! If they had all been buried on that same day, and had made the trip together to the next world. What an exciting "confrontation" that would be.'

Where?

Before Muhammad, of course, the Founder of Islam.

They excuse all *their* crimes and atrocities against the Bahá'ís because they are enemies of Islam. Wouldn't it be rewarding to know how Muhammad feels about it? Wouldn't it be rewarding to see all of them together before Him, face to face. And let the Apostle of God, Himself, hear both sides of the story, then choose between them.

Who was the *servant,* and who was the *enemy* of Islam? In Teheran on that tragic Monday.

As a sportscaster, I'd lay the odds at 'one-to-nine-on' that the 'antagonistic' group of 'terrorists' would get the short end of the stick, and leave dishonoured and in disgrace.

My money would be on Dr Manúchihr Ḥakím.

Except that Baná'ís don't gamble.

Pity!

It would have been a 'sure thing'!

4

Another cablegram!

This time about Teheran.

They had executed three Baná'ís on the twenty-second of June, and four more on the twenty-third.

1981!

I have not typed out the cablegram for you this time. Both of us must be weary by now of that song of death.

To the growing list of fatalities, all victims of '*Terrible Teheran*', must now be added seven more innocent servants of humanity: peace-loving, law-abiding, non-violent – like an inescapable refrain it is heard again and again, running through our story with the melody of death.

The story of each one of these heroes of God should be told in detail. And will be some day.

Yes, believe it or not, I *did* know them. Some of them very closely. They are part of my Bahá'í family. I am suffering along with their own relatives.

The memories were flowing so strongly that at home in Canada after that phone call, I put up my portable movie screen, and looked again at the beautiful coloured slides I had taken in Teheran of those places and people so dear to my heart. My memories were mingled with joy and sadness. Joy at the victories, sadness at the terrible suffering now being inflicted on my fellow Bahá'ís.

I had taken coloured slides and photographs of our Conferences and consultations together in that very city, Teheran, where they now lay dead. Counsellor, Auxiliary Board member, outstanding servants of the Faith of Bahá'u'lláh.

I flashed on the screen the coloured slide of the lovely face of Counsellor Dr Masíḥ Farhangí, a sweet and darling soul, a true lover of his fellow men, a close personal friend. I would now add his name to the list of the crimes of 'Terrible Teheran'.

I turned the projector off and the screen was empty. Like my heart. Something precious had vanished.

They are all dear, all loved, and all missed. They died, shot to death, while I was writing this book.

> Dr Masíḥ Farhangí
> Mr Háshim Farnúsh
> Mr Buzurg 'Alavíyán
> Mr Farhang Mavaddat

Mr Badí'u'lláh Faríd
Mr Yadu'lláh Pústchí
Mr Varqá Tibyáníyán

The names of these new victims have been listed for you not only to show that the systematic killings are still going on, but also to point out once again that these Bahá'í murders are *not,* as is so often inferred in the press, part of the general executions taking place in Iran during the current Islamic Revolution.

That, of course, is exactly the impression the present regime is trying to convey. They are hoping that the obliteration of the entire Bahá'í community in Iran can be accomplished without being noticed in the midst of all the current confusion.

These murders are *not* part of anything. How many times I have said that! They are a separate, carefully conceived, cunningly executed, systematic, deadly plan to exterminate the Bahá'í community in Iran behind the smoke-screen of the Islamic Revolution.

Repeat:

It may be a Revolution, but it certainly is not Islamic. These unjust murders are completely against everything Muhammad taught.

The Bahá'ís are *not* unfortunate victims caught accidentally in the web of historical circumstances.

They are intended victims of genocide!

Deliberate. Planned. Unrelenting.

5

It is time to say farewell to 'Terrible Teheran'.

The religious leaders in Iran, who should be the most God-fearing, honoured, respected, charitable, kindly and considerate of *all* men, are instead, through their terrorists, the betrayer, the executioner, the axe and the headman's block all rolled into one.

They, alone, must accept the full world-wide responsibility and shame for the innocent Bahá'í blood they have shed.

Never before have they had such a perfect opportunity to accomplish their one-hundred-and-fifty-year-old goal. Up until now, their greatest opportunity was in 1852 when they were able to gain the full support and assistance of the civil government under Nasiri'd-Din Shah.

That almost perfect attempt at genocide failed.

They are trying again today.

Conditions look more favourable now.

If the safety and lives of my friends in Iran were not at stake, I would skip the ferocity and horror of those days back in 1852. But I have no other choice.

This is the persecution, the 'grand butchery' described by the renowned French author, Ernest Renan, as 'a day without parallel, perhaps, in the history of the world'.

You have a right to know about it.

This brief glimpse into the past will also prove to you, once and for all, that I was telling you the truth when I said that these terrorists now deployed in Iran, are torturemongers from the Stone Age.

They were then; they are now.

I believe you will also agree that my language, as I suggested in the beginning, was not too strong, but was in reality, mild and moderate.

I leave it to you.

We have chosen to share with you at this point an account not written by the Bahá'ís, but written by an Austrian soldier and published in *Soldatenfreund* (The Soldier's Friend) on that terrible occasion nearly one hundred and fifty years ago.

Fasten your seat-belts for a flight to hell and beyond!

6

On August 29, 1852, Captain Alfred von Gumoens, an

Austrian officer in the service of Nasiri'd-Din Shah, wrote a letter to a friend. He was so 'disgusted and horrified at the cruelties he was compelled to witness that he sent in his resignation'.

You can read the entire letter for yourself in the files of *Oesterreichischer Soldatenfreund* in the reference libraries of Austria, or in *The Dawn-Breakers,* pp. 605-6, which any Bahá'í in your town will be happy to share with you.*

Both you and I will be equally as disgusted as Captain von Gumoens; so I have shortened his account of those horrors for the sake of us all.

[Teheran, August 29, 1852]
... But follow me, my friend, you who lay claim to a heart and European ethics, follow me to the unhappy ones who, with gouged-out eyes, ... whose teeth are torn out with inhuman violence by the hand of the executioner; or whose bare skulls are simply crushed by blows from a hammer; or where the bazaar is illuminated with unhappy victims, because on right and left the people dig deep holes in their breasts and shoulders and insert burning wicks [of candles] in the wounds. I saw some dragged in chains through the bazaar, preceded by a military band ...

They will skin the soles of [their] feet, soak the wounds in boiling oil, shoe the foot like the hoof of a horse, and compel the victim to run ... Give him the *coup de grâce*! Put him out of his pain! No! The executioner swings the whip, and – I myself have had to witness it – the unhappy victim of hundred-fold tortures runs! ... As for the end itself, they hang the scorched and perforated bodies by their hands and feet to a tree head-downwards, and now every Persian may try his marksmanship to his heart's content ... I saw corpses torn by nearly 150 bullets ...

When I read over again what I have written I am

* The complete letter can also be found in *The Bábí and Bahá'í Religions, 1844–1944,* pp. 132–4 (see p. 30 for details).

overcome by the thought that those who are with you in
our dearly beloved Austria may doubt the full truth of
the picture, and accuse me of exaggeration. Would to
God that I had not lived to see it. But by the duties of
my profession I was unhappily often, only too often, a
witness of these abominations. At present I never leave
my house, in order not to meet with fresh scenes of
horror. After their death the [victims] are hacked in two
and either nailed to the city gate, or cast out into the
plain as food for the dogs and jackals . . .

Since my whole soul revolts against such infamy,
against such abominations . . . I will no longer maintain
my connection with the scene of such crimes.

Captain von Gumoens goes on to say that he has
already asked for his discharge, but has not yet received
an answer.

We can summarize that day in 1852, 'without parallel . . . in the history of the world', and be finished with it,
by briefly quoting one more historical document of those
events.

'Those arrested were distributed among the various
classes of people, whose messengers would visit the
dungeon each day and claim their victims.'

It was the Prime Minister's idea. He feared that he
alone might be blamed for these inhuman atrocities.
Therefore, in order to distribute the responsibility, he
conceived the extraordinary idea of distributing these
poor, helpless souls among the various classes of people,
each having its own victim.

They were divided as equally and fairly as possible
among the Clergy, Ministers of State, the Army, the
Doctors of Law, the chief servants of the Court, the
people of the town, merchants, tradesmen and artisans.

One example from the endless parade of horrendous
killings will be more than enough.

The Minister of Foreign Affairs, 'full of religious and
moral zeal, took the first shot'. He was given one of the

more illustrious victims, as befitted his position in the Government, and the secretaries of his department finished the victim off, and then cut him to pieces before returning to their offices to get on with the day's work.

All this information is from an article published in the *Teheran Gazette*.

And still they would not say:

'I am not a Bahá'í.'

They *were* Bahá'ís.

Once Bahá'u'lláh had touched their hearts, they would always be Bahá'ís. To be a follower of Bahá'u'lláh is more precious than life itself. Because it *is* life itself. Everything else is ashes.

Captain von Gumoens left 'Terrible Teheran' shortly after. Forever. Can you really blame him?

8

Hamadan

'Can it really be Hamadan?'

It had been a peaceful day. No cablegrams, no telephone calls. I sighed a breath of relief, and prepared for bed. I had put in a long day typing disasters and calamities. The quiet was restful.

There was a loud knock upon my door! A messenger from Toronto. Delivering another telex cablegram. This one dated June 14, 1981. Yesterday!

Another seven dead.

The cable was from Hamadan, Iran.

Hamadan!

One of my favourite places in all that land. Ecbatana of the Greeks. The great philosopher and physician, Avicenna is buried there. As is the poet Baba Tahir, grandson of Omar Khayyam. Alexander the Great once captured the city. Herodotus wrote about it. Darius I, and Artaxerxes II, raised up royal structures there.

I mention all these things about Hamadan, merely to put off facing the words of my cablegram.

SEVEN BAHA'IS ALL MEMBERS OF THE LOCAL SPIRITUAL ASSEMBLY OF HAMADAN WERE TORTURED AND KILLED TODAY JUNE 14, 1981

The tortures they endured were discovered as their bodies were being prepared for burial. I must now add to my list of lost loved ones and friends:

Mr Ḥusayn Muṭlaq
Shot nine times by the executioner

Mr Suhayl Ḥabíbí
Shoulder broken. Shot

Mr Suhráb Ḥabíbí
Back burned. Branded. Shot five times

Dr Náṣir Vafá'í
Thighs cut open as far as his waist. Shot twice

Dr Fírúz Na'ímí
Back broken. Shot seven times

Mr Ḥusayn Khándil
Fingers crushed. Back burned. Branded. Shot

Mr Ṭarázu'lláh Khuzayn
Chest and left hand smashed. Shot seven times

Hamadan, a city of history of the past, is now a city of murder in the present.

As I sit here at my typewriter in the safety and peace of Canada, my heart is restless. I find it hard to sleep at night. I keep thinking of those dear faces in Hamadan.

I am watching two graceful Canadian geese, back from the south for the summer, gliding smoothly along the surface of the blue pond below my window. I am surrounded by green fields, meadows of flowers, and dark pines. The smell of jasmine floats through the open window. I can hear the soothing sound of the swift-flowing waters of the Ganaraska River spilling over the mill-race and dam below. But no matter how I try to endure the unendurable, every few minutes my heart goes back to the land of nightingales and blue tile fountains, Iran.

And to Hamadan!

How I would like to share the tranquillity and beauty of my gardener's cottage with the dear families of the survivors in Hamadan in their hour of anguish and suffering.

The cablegram tells me how my Bahá'í friends were arrested, imprisoned, interrogated – all illegally. How they were offered their freedom if they would recant, and how they refused. As an inducement, they were tortured. They still refused.

They were killed with the sanction, approval and blessing of the local authorities, as well as the approval of the highest Revolutionary Court in the land.

There was only one slight annoyance for the enemies. The members of the hated Local Spiritual Assembly of Hamadan stood fast to the very end. The cruel tortures inflicted on them only stiffened their resolve.

I remember Hamadan, and the dear sweet people I met there. I spoke to several hundred Bahá'ís in their beautiful Centre. I met with the Local Spiritual Assembly for a wonderful lunch and dinner. Seven of the nine are gone now.

Oh, yes! I remember all my friends. Not *only* those in Hamadan.

How often does one person have such dear and tender friends killed in Tabriz, Shiraz, Yazd, Teheran, and now Hamadan?

I can see the shining, radiant faces of the members of that Local Spiritual Assembly on the day we met, as if it were yesterday. First, we sat down together for a Persian dinner. I can still smell the fragrant, wonderful Persian feast they served. It was a work of art laid out before us on the long table heaped with delicious delicacies.

I remember *chilau fisinján*, *Khurisht-i-bádinjan*. There is no chicken in the world more tasty. *Mast va Khiyar*, *Kharbozeh*, *Talebi*, melons of such fragrance – on and on went the wonders. The food was only surpassed by the love and hospitality of all our hosts and hostesses in Hamadan, and all the dear believers.

Most of all, I remember the people. Their laughter and

fellowship. A little round-faced boy just learning to talk. His big black saucer-eyes flashing as he giggled every time I looked at him. He kept saying; '*Khudá Háfíz*', 'Goodbye', instead of 'Hello'. Even when he was hugging my knees in welcome.

Everybody was radiant, sparkling, filled with happiness. Bahá'í friends from across the seas in America had come to Hamadan to visit.

I can still picture the very dignified Bahá'í who read from the Bahá'í writings at the start of our meeting.

When the reading was finished, I whispered to my nearest neighbour. '*Fársí-i-man khub níst.* (My Persian is not good.) Translate for me, please.'

He did. I could see that he knew the passage by heart. So did I. I recognized it the moment he began.

> They who are the people of God have no ambition except to revive the world, to ennoble its life, and regenerate its peoples. Truthfulness and good-will have, at all times, marked their relations with all men. Their outward conduct is but a reflection of their inward life, and their inward life a mirror of their outward conduct.

Those were happy, unforgettable hours in Hamadan.

At the close of our meeting that evening, another dear Bahá'í, also a member of the Local Spiritual Assembly, ended our session by reading one of my favourite prayers.

It was from the pen of Bahá'u'lláh, Founder of the Bahá'í Faith. It was recited in English, in my honour. It was my farewell to Hamadan.

> O Thou Who art the Lord of Lords! ... I bear witness that Thy power hath encompassed the entire universe, and that the hosts of the earth can never dismay Thee, nor can the dominion of all peoples and nations deter Thee from executing Thy purpose. I confess that Thou hast no desire except the regeneration of the whole

world, and the establishment of the unity of its peoples, and the salvation of all them that dwell therein.

Well done, Hamadan.

Tabriz, Teheran, Shiraz and Yazd salute you!

The efforts made to suppress the Bahá'í Faith and to obliterate its name from the face of the country produced exactly the opposite result in Hamadan. Because of the heroic martyrdoms there, the Faith of Bahá'u'lláh was proclaimed, as never before, to the frustration and fury of the persecutors.

So prevalent was the proclamation of the Faith in this city of some 200,000 inhabitants, so forceful the indignation and condemnation of the persecutions voiced by both Muslims and Bahá'ís alike, that a religious judge took to the airwaves, to television, to denounce such behaviour. He warned that anyone who continued to sympathize with this false religion would be punished.

He repeated all the old familiar false charges levied against the Bahá'í community, hoping by his intimidation to bring to an abrupt end this wave of protest and sympathy which the actions of the torturers and persecutors had aroused by their cruel treatment of the seven Bahá'í martyrs.

From the very first day of their imprisonment eleven months ago, these heroes of Hamadan had openly declared their willingness, nay their eagerness, to give their lives for their Faith. When the day came, they were abruptly told of their imminent execution, to take place almost immediately. They proceeded to bathe, shave, put on their best clothes, and to make themselves fragrant with cologne and attar-of-rose. They were preparing to meet their Lord.

Their fellow inmates, Muslims, who had come to admire, respect and grow very fond of these cheerful, courageous Bahá'ís, wept as they watched their new-found friends preparing so calmly for their deaths. The

Bahá'í prisoners consoled them, and in a state of complete serenity bade them a final farewell.

On Sunday morning at 3.00 a.m., a Bahá'í woman, working at the Government Hospital, was informed that the bodies of the seven martyrs of Hamadan had been transferred there. The bodies had been thrown, roughly and callously, one on top of the other, like a pile of discarded laundry.

By 8.30 that same morning, a crowd of Bahá'ís, and many who were not Bahá'ís, had gathered on the Hospital grounds. Their number was rapidly increasing and became so large and restless that the Hospital gates were closed, shutting the people outside.

The crowd was still growing, sharing the grief and tears of the Bahá'ís at the news of the tragic events that had taken place. The Muslims were shocked at the cruelty and disgraceful treatment which had been inflicted upon these seven Bahá'í victims. They said so.

The Bahá'ís requested an ambulance to transport their fallen heroes to the cemetery. Their request was refused.

'The ambulance', they were told, 'is only for the use of patients.'

Appeals to the cemetery authorities, and finally to the provincial Government, were all denied. No one would help.

The Muslims present were very upset at this heartless injustice and hostility. They urged the Bahá'ís to protest. Carry the bodies of your dead to the middle of Hamadan, they advised, and demonstrate loudly against these cruel acts.

'You are justified!' they insisted.

The Bahá'ís told them that, as Bahá'ís, they were law-abiding, peace-loving, and loyal to their government. They would obey, however unjust and painful the cruel restrictions against them might be.

'If we cannot secure an ambulance,' the Bahá'ís told the

crowd, 'we shall carry our martyrs upon our shoulders to the Bahá'í cemetery.'

Because of the delays, the crowd of people gathered outside the Hospital gate grew larger. The crush became so threatening that finally, because of the insistence and loud clamour of the crowd, the gates were opened. They flooded into the Hospital grounds.

Mrs Muṭlaq, the wife of one of the martyrs, stood on a stool and delivered a moving and eloquent speech about the seven who had just died so gallantly. Perfectly calm and composed, with no criticism of the authorities whatsoever, Mrs Muṭlaq explained the Bahá'í principles and the fundamental truths of the Faith, for which her husband and his six companions had given their lives.

'These seven innocent men', she said, 'have shed their blood so that the hearts of all men everywhere can be washed clean, and freed from all hatred and enmity.'

Her words penetrated the hearts of the crowd, and were well received.

Another Bahá'í woman began to chant a Bahá'í prayer in a loud, clear and melodious voice. The large crowd listened in absolute silence. Even the employees and staff of the hospital had stopped work, and gathered to listen to both the talk and the prayer. One of the ambulance drivers was so moved by what he heard, that he volunteered his own ambulance to transfer the seven martyrs to the Bahá'í cemetery.

Those precious bodies, still clad in their blood-stained clothes, and in full view of the crowd, were placed lovingly inside the ambulance. Slowly, it set out for the Bahá'í cemetery.

Muslims and Bahá'ís were deeply touched by the scene. Spontaneously they began to applaud, as they cried out the praises of God.

'Alláh-u-Akbar!'

'Alláh-u-Abhá!'

In such dramatic and thrilling manner, in a united

expression of love and unity, the sombre procession passed through the hospital gates, and began its journey toward the final resting-place of those seven innocent victims.

The ambulance, and its huge retinue of mourners who moved solemnly in its wake, passed through one of the poorer sections of Hamadan. Shopkeepers closed their doors, came out into the street, and joined the great multitude of mourners. They asked *why* these men had been killed. What had they done? They were curious and deeply touched by the great show of love and respect for the fallen heroes. All their questions were answered, as the solemn procession wound its way through the city.

It was a day of proclamation such as Hamadan had not seen since the historic days of Ṭáhirih. The door had been opened by the deaths of these seven brave soldiers in the 'radiant spiritual Army of Bahá'u'lláh'!

As they neared the cemetery, people came out of the nearby houses and joined the funeral procession. They, too, were told what had happened and why. They, likewise, were indignant and angered. By the time the funeral cortège reached the Bahá'í cemetery, the procession was two kilometres long. There, in the cemetery, as preparations for the final interment began, the questions and the answers about the Bahá'í Faith continued unabated. For every Bahá'í present on that occasion, there were *ten* Muslims.

As those precious bodies were being washed and prepared for burial, the tortures which they had been forced to endure were plain for everyone to see. The record of the inhuman treatment, to which they had all been subjected, was written on their broken bodies.

Some of the Muslims who, at first, had come mostly out of curiosity, pressed forward to see the wounds for themselves. They were outraged at what they beheld. They cursed the authorities who had perpetrated these hideous, cruel acts. Quickly they went among the Muslim crowd to tell what they had seen. They, themselves, they said, were eyewitnesses to the barbarous behaviour of the Hamadan authorities. A commotion began to stir among the crowd. Other Muslim visitors pushed their way forward to see for themselves if these rumours were true.

They were.

Some of the Muslim sympathizers went so far as to leave the cemetery, and return with their relatives and friends. They wanted them to behold, with their own eyes, the ruthless persecutions which had been inflicted upon those victims of hatred.

During the reading of the prayer for the dead, members of the crowd, who were not Bahá'ís, quickly learned the verses and joined in the chanting of the repetitive parts of the Bahá'í text. The final interment took place before sunset that same day.

It was indeed a time of unique proclamation for Hamadan. It had foiled every plan of the persecutors, and the death of the seven heroes had been triumphant.

9

Shiraz

No one in Iran has yet devised a more economical way to add to his own property and possessions than by confiscation, however illegally, of Bahá'í resources.

I spent happy hours and happy days with the Bahá'ís in Shiraz, visiting their beautiful Centre with its trees, flowers, gardens, and lovely paths. Confiscated now. Vandalized, looted, then occupied by the Revolutionary authorities for their own use.

The executions in Shiraz have now stretched out over a three-year period. They culminated in the murder of five Bahá'ís in March and April of this year, 1981.

The story of each one of these heroes of God would make a novel by itself. Each story is filled with the necessary ingredients: suspense, drama, hate, love, sacrifice, and finally death. They will *all* be told, again and again, in the future.

The story of each one is being recorded for the annals of Shiraz:

> Mr Yadu'lláh Vaḥdat
> Mr Sattár <u>Kh</u>ushkhú
> Mr Iḥsánu'lláh Mihdí-Zádih
> Mr Mihdí Anvarí
> Mr Hidáyatu'lláh Dihqání

The account of the deaths of the two Bahá'ís from Abadih who were executed in Shiraz gives yet another proof of the indomitable courage of these martyrs in the face of the brutality and viciousness, both mental and physical, of the torturers assigned to kill them.

The execution of Hidáyatu'lláh Dihqání and Mihdí Anvarí created a stir among the people of Shiraz, both Bahá'ís and non-Bahá'ís. Until the very last moment of their lives the Revolutionary Guards had hammered at them time and again to induce them to recant their Faith. It is the favourite game of the various religious regimes in Iran, a killer's game that has been played for nearly one hundred and fifty years.

'You can be freed,' they were told. 'We'll call off the execution. You can live, not die. You can go back to your wives and children. Safe and free.'

They both refused.

So the execution began.

But the executioners were not finished with their cunning tortures. They still hoped to force a recantation from these two brave men by resorting to surprise and terror, hoping to break their spirits at the last moment. All the preliminary preparations for the final execution were completed. The victims braced themselves to die for the Faith they loved. They were offering prayers of thanksgiving for being given this special honour. The guns were raised, the order given, the guns fired. Everything was carried out precisely.

Except for one thing.

The executioners deliberately missed their victims. They were not struck by the bullets even though their bodies may have flinched at the sound of the gunfire. The guns had been fired into the air. It was a mock execution designed to break down the resistance of the two victims, to frighten Anvarí and Dihqání into saying at last that, since they had had this chance to think it over, they were not Bahá'ís after all. It was hoped they would recant, rather than go through that scene of death all over again.

The cruel tactics backfired. It only stiffened the resolve of these two courageous men.

'Will you recant now?'

'Never!'

The Revolutionary Guards offered them one last chance to denounce their Faith. One of those dear souls said calmly in reply:

'Our Beloved [the Báb] received seven hundred and fifty of your bullets. Why should we fear your three or four!'

Frustrated, infuriated, and foiled in all their attempts, the executioners finally carried out their murderous work.

Mr Anvarí, as a last wish, asked his family to distribute sweets among those who had executed them, so that he might thank them for the privilege of dying for his religion. The family carried out his request. They offered money rather than sweets. They did not want to know who the executioner of their husband and father had been.

The families, the Bahá'í survivors, were staunch and courageous in the face of continuing difficulties and harassment. In answer to a message of sympathy from the World Centre of their Faith, Mr Dihqání's family replied:

'We still have some drops of eager blood in our family, and we are ready to offer them in the path of God whenever it is necessary.'

The daughter of one of these martyrs of Shiraz, an eight-year-old Bahá'í student, was the only child permitted to visit her father on the day of his execution. This little girl, in this same spirit, brought flowers and sweets to distribute to her teacher and classmates. The teacher was surprised. She asked: 'Is it a Bahá'í custom to do such a thing when one's father is killed?'

The little girl replied proudly:

'My father was not killed. He was martyred.'

I love her.

10

Tabriz

1

Still another cablegram!

TABRIZ, JULY 14, 1980, YADU'LLAH ASTANI,
FARAMARZ SAMANDARI CHAIRMAN AND
MEMBER LOCAL ASSEMBLY TABRIZ SHOT TO
DEATH TODAY. DETAILS FOLLOW.

Details followed soon after. Same baseless accusations, trumped-up charges, illegal arrest, imprisonment and execution.

Their crime?

They were members of the Bahá'í Local Spiritual Assembly of Tabriz. A great honour elsewhere in the world. A crime meriting death in Iran.

Yes, I knew them both. I stopped for some time in Tabriz. I met with the Local Spiritual Assembly there, and with all the dear Bahá'í friends in that city.

The Herald of the Bahá'í Faith, the Báb Himself, had been shot to death by a firing-squad in Tabriz, in the same month of July, 131 years before.

Oh yes, the whole Bahá'í world knows about Tabriz. They know in detail about the baseless accusation and false charges which led to the death of these two wonderful men who were servants of their fellow men, their city, and their country, and who did more good for Tabriz than all their accusers combined.

It was growing late. July 14th was almost over. Earlier that night Dr Samandarí and Mr Ástání had been informed that they would die in a few hours.

They prayed and prepared themselves for death.

Both these elected representatives of the Bahá'ís of Tabriz had shed such love upon their fellow prisoners and guards, who were not Bahá'ís, that when these Muslims heard the news that their newly-made friends were to be shot to death, they wept.

At midnight, Yadu'lláh Ástání and Dr Farámarz Samandarí were taken from the prison and led to the scene of their execution. They walked past several of the other prisoners, who had been convicted of drug activity and other crimes. These prisoners, who knew they would soon die themselves, shouted loudly in protest at the Revolutionary Guards and executioners:

'We are guilty!'

'Kill us!'

'But why kill the kind doctor? Why?'

Dr Samandarí had been called at times to the prison infirmary to treat the prisoners. Now, he and his fellow Bahá'í brother, Yadu'lláh Ástání, were to be killed. Whatever false charges may have been announced, they both knew only too well that they were being killed for one reason only.

They were Bahá'ís.

2

There had been little time for Mr Ástání and Dr Samandarí to send a last message of love to their dear ones. They did the best they could. They incorporated their tender goodbyes in their Wills, written as they were about to die.

In almost every case, the heroes and heroines of God have hurriedly written down their last thoughts to their

loved ones. Hastily, abruptly, death came to them suddenly and unexpectedly. The prison authorities still have not surrendered some of these precious Wills to the families and survivors to whom they were written with such tender love.

I want to share with you one of these last precious moments, from the farewell words of an innocent victim of oppression and hate. A hero of this great religious drama being unfolded across the entire face of Iran. There are many like him.

What does the heart say in such a moment?

The photograph shows you the happy and loving family of Dr Farámarz Samandarí of Tabriz. It was taken in happier days, before he was illegally arrested, falsely accused, unlawfully imprisoned, tried, and executed on trumped-up charges. Imagine if you were the darling wife, and had received the following letter, a last letter from the one dearest to you in all the world, one who never again in this world would hold you to his heart.

You were expecting to hear his familiar footstep at the door any minute, free! Everyone knew how wonderful he was, and how utterly false and ridiculous were the charges made against him. Then, suddenly, out of the blue, they told you he was dead. Shot to death for being a lover of his fellow men.

Now, this. A letter. Not your husband, but merely a last remnant of his love.

Or, possibly, you are the husband, the victim of such tyrants.

What then? What would *you* have written to your dear ones in those last fast-fleeting moments of your life?

This is what was written by one of the dearest Bahá'í friends anyone could ever have.

It is taken from the last Will and Testament of Farámarz Samandarí:

In the name of God, the Merciful, the
Compassionate!
'O my God, the All-knowing
Thou art the One Who knowest
the secrets of my heart.'
'Abdu'l-Bahá

After confirming my belief in the Oneness of God
and in the reality of His Messengers including the
prophet Muhammad, and confessing the truth of His
Holiness Bahá'u'lláh, at this moment when I am
spending the last hours of my life in prison, I write
these few lines as my will.

I have committed no crime except being a Bahá'í. I
have sincerely served this country and its people.

All my belongings, movable and immovable which I
have now or I might receive in the future, I leave to my
wife Anita (Carr) Samandarí. So also, with whatever
funds are in my bank accounts. She is free to use them
in whatever way she wishes.

I request that my dear wife Anita do her utmost in
training our children, Kiyumars, Maryam and Kamyar. I apologize to her for leaving her to shoulder the
heavy responsibility of bringing up the children all
alone. I ask my sisters to assist Anita whole-heartedly
in raising our children.

Goodbye my honourable father and mother. Goodbye my dear Anita. Goodbye my dear Kiyumars, dear
Maryam and dear Kamyar. Goodbye my dear sisters,
Farangiz, Mehrangiz, Ruhangiz, Shoorangiz, Simin
and Nasrin. Goodbye my dear Bahá'í and non-Bahá'í
friends.

In two more hours I am to be executed by a firing-
squad together with my dear Bahá'í brother Yadu'lláh
Ástání. I am most grateful to everyone.

Please pray for the progress of my soul.

Signed,
SAMANDARÍ

*[The above statement is certified. Seal of: Prison of Islamic
Revolution of Iran.]*

Bahá'í families in Abadih, Ahram, Andrun-Birjand, Buyr-Ahmad, Bukan, Jahrum, Karaj, Khurasan, Khurmuj, Mahabad, Miyan-Du'ab, Nuk-Birjand, Piranshahr, Rasht, Sanandaj, Shiraz, Tabriz, Teheran, Ushnaviyyih, Urumiyyih, Yazd, and God alone knows in what additional cities of bloodthirsty Iran may, by the time this reaches you, have already read with broken hearts a similar message from a loved one written from a different prison.

Or, as a last insult, these tender words of love, encouragement and farewell, may be held back deliberately by the authorities, so that those dear ones may go to their graves without sharing that last embrace of loving words with their fathers, mothers, wives, sons and daughters.

3

The Iranian Representative to the United Nations said that there was no organized plan to persecute the Bahá'ís in Iran. Less than two weeks later, Yadu'lláh Ástání and Dr Farámarz Samandarí, two Bahá'ís being held in prison, were dead in Tabriz. Suddenly, unexpectedly, someone was sent to Tabriz from Teheran, the capital, to carry out the summary execution order.

It was announced first on the radio, then later the same day on television, that two Bahá'ís, the Chairman and a member of the Bahá'í Local Spiritual Assembly of Tabriz, had been found guilty of crimes against the State.

They were executed for these unknown crimes.

A representative of the Bahá'í community in Iran met with a high official on the same day as that fatal announcement. The official was greatly surprised. He did not know how it happened, but suddenly, out of the blue, came the news that two Bahá'ís had been executed in Tabriz.

No one, especially those in authority, seemed to know

anything at all about an orderly, systematic, and thorough campaign to erase gradually from the face of Iran their single largest religious minority.

Yet the killings went on. Systematically, gradually, and in an orderly fashion. How passing strange!

The charges, however, must have been extremely familiar to everyone, from the Revolutionary Guards to the Revolutionary Courts. The same misrepresentations, false accusations, fraudulent, trumped-up charges appeared again in Tabriz:

1. Conspiring against the Government
2. Spying for Israel
3. Conspiring against the sovereignty of the country
4. Participating in the Bahá'í Conferences in London and New Delhi
5. Plotting against Islam
6. Being involved in immorality and prostitution

The first three charges have already been fully answered. Number four is amusing, isn't it? If it hadn't brought death in its wake.

The authorities have left out the Conferences in Sydney, Singapore, Chicago, Panama City, Merida (Mexico), Nairobi, Stockholm, Frankfurt, Kampala, Hong Kong, Saporro, Auckland, Palermo, Port Louis (Mauritius Island), Helsinki, Reykjavik, and more than a dozen other Bahá'í Conferences whose locations escape me at the moment. These Conferences have been going on for years with the enthusiastic support of the cities in which they were held.

I could look them up, but it seems entirely unnecessary, as the whole world was informed by press, radio, television, and magazine articles about them. They were world-wide gatherings with always the same theme:

1. The oneness and unity of the entire human race.

2. The peace, prosperity and security of all nations, great and small (including Iran).
3. The Bahá'í Message of love and fellowship for people of all races, nations and religions.

Can you believe that, according to their own record, one of the reasons for killing Yadu'lláh Ástání and Dr Farámarz Samandarí was for participating in such Bahá'í Conferences in London and New Delhi?

The World Press in general praised those Bahá'í gatherings as peace-loving and inspiring. Some newspapers gave headlines to those international gatherings:

'WELCOME BAHÁ'ÍS!'

And: 'Please come back!'

Some cities, blessed by these Conferences, reported that they had never seen such an orderly, courteous, non-violent group of people in such great numbers in their cities before.

There were no street riots, no drunken brawls, no acts of vandalism. There were, instead, many stories of hotel managers and bus drivers who were so attracted and pleased by the Bahá'ís assembled in their city that, as a parting gift, they were invited to special free farewell breakfasts, lunches and dinners.

One bus driver took his entire Bahá'í group to his own favourite restaurant for breakfast in his company bus on their final morning, as *his* guests, because he didn't want to say goodbye to the Bahá'ís just yet. The hours he had spent with them, he said, had been too wonderful. Bahá'ís, surely, were quite different from the rest of the peoples of the world.

Everyone who came in contact with the Bahá'í spirit on those occasions felt good! Even the prisoners and guards in Tabriz prison on that fatal midnight had felt this love radiating from Yadu'lláh Ástání and Dr Farámarz Samandarí.

A representative of the International Red Cross, who

visited Tabriz prison, later reported that he remembered seeing two Bahá'ís in prison in Tabriz 'who were very nice and well-liked, even by the prison authorities'.

The writings of the Bahá'í Faith say clearly and unequivocally that Bahá'ís everywhere in the world must be lovers of mankind. These are the superior people of whatever country, creed or colour they may be.

At every great International Bahá'í Conference, the followers of Bahá'u'lláh are motivated by these words, instructions from the Bahá'í writings telling them how they must behave among the people of the world. There are no exceptions:

> I charge you all that each one of you concentrate all the thoughts of your heart on love and unity. When a thought of war comes, oppose it by a stronger thought of peace. A thought of hatred must be destroyed by a more powerful thought of love ...
> If you desire with all your heart friendship with every race on earth, your thought, spiritual and positive, will spread; it will become the desire of others, growing stronger and stronger, until it reaches the minds of all men.

Dr Samandarí and Yadu'lláh Ástání, at the New Delhi and London Bahá'í Conferences, along with their thousands and thousands of Bahá'í brothers and sisters from the five races of mankind, were 'alive with plans to dedicate the rest of their lives to the welfare and betterment of mankind'.

They were prepared to die for it.

They did!

The spirit of every Bahá'í Conference, such as those in London and New Delhi, can be found in these words from the Bahá'í writings:

> All peoples and nations are of one family, the children of one Father [God], and should be to one another as

brothers and sisters! I hope that you will endeavour in your lives to show forth and spread this teaching.

Man should be gentle, 'but when he becomes ferocious he is more cruel and malicious than the most savage of the animal creation!'

Yadu'lláh Ástání and Dr Farámarz Samandarí found that to be true in the city of Tabriz.

4

We cannot leave Tabriz without dealing directly with the false charge that *Yadu'lláh Ástání and Dr Farámarz Samandarí were involved in immorality and prostitution.*

Let me begin by saying that to anyone even the least familiar with the Bahá'í Faith such an accusation is both asinine and fatuous. This charge is the utter, absolute, depraved limit.

I said earlier that this book would not be a dignified White Paper to be presented to governments, nor a calm, reasoned diplomatic response for United Nations Conferences. It is exactly what the title says it is: *A Cry from the Heart*! So my non-violent fury and peaceful indignation have to leak out once in a while. I'll try to keep them under control.

But *not* right now.

I'm not used to having dearly-loved and close friends strangled, stabbed, stoned, set on fire, and shot down for no reason at all except that they were Bahá'ís, the most wonderful thing in the world they could possibly be, if they wanted to be helpful to their fellow men.

The present regime in Iran says they are not being killed because of their religion, that many people are being executed for many reasons, all criminal, as part of the great Islamic Revolution.

I repeat, that the killing of my Bahá'í friends is not a

part of anything. It is a separate, pre-arranged plan of genocide. It has been from the start.

It is only the Bahá'ís in Iran who, in all parts of the country, are being systematically, regularly, and ruthlessly slain, according to this well-planned attempt to do away with them all behind the smoke-screen of the Islamic Revolution.

I *know* you've heard this several times, but not half as often as the world has heard the present regime in Iran say, 'They are not killed because they are Bahá'ís, but because they are criminals.'

I say, 'Rubbish!'

I should have a stamp made of my views, and just bang it down on the page every now and then. Or, I could have one of my musician friends compose a theme song for them called:

'Which side is your side? Homicide or genocide?'

All right! So it's sarcastic.

Is it any worse than tying a farmer's darling wife to a wooden door, soaking her with kerosene, and setting her ablaze?

You have read *her* story.

Somebody, somewhere, sometime, should have the right to say: 'Shame! Crime! Killer loose on the innocent!'

Fair is fair.

I didn't write this book to throw bouquets of roses at them for murder and arson. I'd be ashamed of myself if I *didn't* cry killer! And then found that they'd slyly, cunningly, and inexorably done away with every Local Assembly member, their wives, their families, and their friends before the world really believed they were murderous animals.

'Hey! What that sportscaster was telling us was true!'

Pity!

I hope the editor leaves all these comments in the book. I wouldn't want you to miss them.

Storm's over. Calm.

To be honest, this is all a prelude to one of the foulest and most evil of all their persecutions thus far. Against all Bahá'í families. In fact, it was this fresh insult to decency that brought on the above outburst. Not content with killing Bahá'ís and destroying their Holy Places, they have come up with a new abomination.

They are going to murder Bahá'í marriages!

I mean it. You won't believe what you're about to read, but it's true. Every word.

I apologize to the families of Yadu'lláh Ástání and Dr Farámarz Samandarí for even dignifying this accusation with an answer, but in the hope of 'awakening the dead' in the various Departments of the authorities in Tabriz, I shall take up and refute their next groundless charge against these two innocent souls.

Actually, these charges of immorality go back as far as 138 years, to the very beginning of the Faith. The Báb Himself was accused of spreading immorality. This baseless accusation was trumped up as long ago as that. The crudity of purpose was readily apparent to the historians of those days. They were not Bahá'ís, not followers of the Báb, not Persian; they were European. These historians knew that the enemies of the Báb were quite capable of manufacturing whatever false charges they felt were necessary in order to undermine the Báb with the people, and thus enable them, eventually, to kill Him.

And they *did* so.

The unbiased reports of outsiders who were privileged to review the character and life of the Báb have said that the 'morality' and 'ethics' He exemplified were above reproach. Here is a statement by Edward Granville Browne in his Notes to *A Traveller's Narrative*:

Of the extraordinary purity and piety of the Báb's life, indeed, we have ample evidence. His bitterest enemies cannot asperse his personal character.

Lord Curzon in his *Persia and the Persian Question*
pointed out:

> At the present time the [followers of the Báb] are
> equally loyal with any other subjects of the
> Crown ... The charge of immorality seems to have
> arisen partly from the malignant inventions of oppo-
> nents, partly from the much greater freedom claimed
> for women by the Bab, which in the oriental mind is
> scarcely dissociable from profligacy of conduct ...
> Broadly regarded, [the Faith of the Báb] may be
> defined as a creed of charity, and almost of common
> humanity. Brotherly love, kindness to children, cour-
> tesy combined with dignity, sociability, hospitality,
> freedom from bigotry, friendliness ... are included in
> its tenets.

The same was said by the friends of Dr Samandarí and
Mr Ástání 131 years later. In almost exactly the same
words:

'The morality and ethics of these two prisoners are
above reproach.'

Everyone – Bahá'ís and non-Bahá'ís alike – fully
expected them both to be released as innocent of all the
charges. They were, of course, not tried on the charges.
Nor were they killed because of them.

You *know* why they were killed.

This false accusation of 'immorality' against the
Bahá'ís has its roots in the fact that, in accordance with
the Bahá'í principle of complete and unquestioned
equality of the sexes, there is no segregation of men and
women during Bahá'í meetings or prayers.

Furthermore, women, as well as men, serve on Bahá'í
administrative institutions, and participate on a basis of
complete equality in all the local and national activities of
the Bahá'í community.

In order to activate this century-and-a-half-old accusation the fanatics in Iran have adopted some of their
cruellest measures of persecution. They have found a new

way to justify their current charges of immorality and
prostitution, and have used these totally false charges as
part of the reasons for killing and debasing two pure-
hearted, honourable family men whose lives were filled
with an integrity and decency which murderers seldom
recognize, and never possess. Especially those who
assassinate character as well as body.

Iran recognizes the marriage of the Jewish, Christian
and Zoroastrian Faiths. They refuse to recognize or
legalize the marriages of the Bahá'ís – the largest single
religious minority in the country, with more members
than all the other three religious minorities combined.

Since they do not recognize Bahá'í marriages, any
father, mother, husband, wife, son or daughter who is part
of such a condemned illegal marriage is immoral,
profligate, defiled, and guilty of the spread of prostitution,
or illegitimate.

This cruel misrepresentation of the true facts of Bahá'í
marriage shames the father, the mother, and the children
before the public. They are insulted on the streets, in the
bazaars, the shopping centres, wherever they go. Sly and
foul comments can be heard, until no mother wishes to
take her children where they can be subject to such vile
remarks.

The children suffer enough as it is at school, those who
haven't already been expelled. They are often beaten,
always harassed. The husbands and wives are branded as
adulterous if they remain together. They are accused of
fostering adultery in their community by being seen
together.

The wives are considered as prostitutes, the husbands
as adulterers, and prostitutes cannot mingle with adulterers in public. The law and decree say it is a crime,
punishable by imprisonment.

It is another string to the enemies' bow, one that carries
the arrow of extermination directly to their Bahá'í target.

The authorities are determined that there shall be no

legal Bahá'í families anywhere in Iran. Every member of the family of this illegal minority religion is thus, one way or another, a criminal, merely by being a father, mother, uncle, aunt, grandfather, or grandmother.

No need to carry the madness any further. Everyone knows the secret purpose.

The present regime in Iran has, in this way, deliberately cast mud at one of the most sacred elements of Bahá'í life: marriage and the family. It is important for us to examine this aspect, not to answer the obviously false charges, but to demonstrate the cruel brutality of any regime that would deprive the world of such beauty as Bahá'í marriage.

For the first time in religious history, the Founder of a religion has Himself given the words which the bride and groom will speak, at the moment of their marriage, words to bind the two lovers together in a holy and lasting relationship as husband and wife, father and mother.

Bahá'u'lláh wishes for them a beautiful, sanctified, enduring and fruitful life. And He, the Founder of the religion, has Himself participated. It is as unique as it is thrilling.

The marriage ceremony can be as modest or as elaborate as the couple may wish, but the heart and soul of it all – the everlasting tie which binds husband and wife together – are the simple words, the brief and significant marriage vows which Bahá'u'lláh Himself, God's Messenger for today, has given to the bride and groom to bless and consecrate that union eternally.

Can you imagine the thrill which Christian, Buddhist, or Muslim bride and groom would feel if they knew that the vows they were about to take had been given to them by Christ Himself, or Buddha, or Muhammad?

Bahá'í marriage is as spiritual, beautiful, and inspiring as any human relationship the world has yet seen. How could it be otherwise? For Bahá'u'lláh has emphasized that we are all the sons and daughters of one Father, God.

He is the Father of all His human family. Therefore, Bahá'u'lláh tells us, the family, the basic unit of society, upon which a strong home, a strong city, a strong nation, a strong world depend must partake of this same spirit of love and unity.

If, the next time the terrorists in Iran break into and vandalize the Bahá'í Centre in Tabriz and confiscate all the documents, they will look under the initial 'M' – for 'Marriage', they will find the answer to their cruel and baseless charge of adultery. They will find the following instruction for the guidance of all Bahá'ís: 'Sex relationships outside marriage are not permissible', and whoso violates this rule 'will suffer severe spiritual deprivation' and be 'responsible to God'.

Furthermore, the Bahá'í writings add: 'Bahá'u'lláh says adultery retards the progress of the soul in the after life – so grievous is it – [thus] we see how clear are our [Bahá'í] teachings on these subjects.'

The Bahá'í Faith clearly and specifically denounces immorality and debased standards of behaviour, saying to every Bahá'í in the world:

> The Bahá'í community must demonstrate in ever-increasing measure its ability to redeem the disorderliness, the lack of cohesion, the permissiveness, the godlessness of modern society; the laws, the religious obligations, the observances of Bahá'í life, Bahá'í moral principles and standards of dignity, decency and reverence, must become deeply implanted in Bahá'í consciousness and increasingly inform and characterize this community.

Bahá'u'lláh has Himself revealed special prayers for marriage so that the husband and wife may keep their wedlock ever green and fragrant.

The following words are a general statement about Bahá'í marriage, and will set at rest the hearts of the

families of those who have been condemned and slain for
believing in its beauty:

> The bond that unites hearts most perfectly is loyalty.
> True lovers once united must show forth the utmost
> faithfulness one to another. You must dedicate your
> knowledge, your talents, your fortunes, ... your bodies
> and your spirits to God, to Bahá'u'lláh, and to each
> other.
>
> Allow no trace of jealousy to creep between you, for
> jealousy, like unto poison, vitiates the very essence of
> love. Let not the ephemeral incidents and accidents of
> this changeful life cause a rift between you. When
> differences present themselves, take counsel together in
> secret, lest others magnify a speck into a mountain.
> Harbour not in your hearts any grievance, but rather
> explain its nature to each other with such frankness and
> understanding that it will disappear, leaving no remem-
> brance. Choose fellowship and amity and turn away
> from jealousy and hypocrisy ...
>
> Let your hearts be like unto two pure mirrors
> reflecting the stars of the heaven of love and beauty ...
>
> No mortal can conceive the union and harmony
> which God has designed for man and wife. Nourish
> continually the tree of your union with love and
> affection, so that it will remain ever green and verdant
> throughout all seasons and bring forth luscious fruits
> for the healing of the nations.

Hide your face in shame, Tabriz! July 14, 1980, was not
only the day you took the lives of two decent, pure-
hearted, innocent men; it was also the day you tried to kill
love and beauty and sweetness and decency, and mortally
wound every family.

Every honourable man and woman who walks the face
of the earth is ashamed of you!

Especially brides and grooms, fathers and mothers, and
all their children. *Shame!*

TABRIZ SPECIAL REPORT

I was taking this manuscript to the editors, and had just stepped off the plane, when I was handed another cablegram.

A report from Tabriz.

Seven more members of the Local Spiritual Assembly of Tabriz had been shot to death, July 29, 1981, together with a member of the Auxiliary Board, and another member of the Bahá'í community of that city.

There were public denials following the outcry against these further killings. These denials, made in both the press and on the radio, stated that there was no special, systematic, organized plan of persecution against the Bahá'í community in Iran. The authorities insisted that Bahá'ís were not killed because of their religion, but because they were criminals. But the authorities, because of pressure from the outside world, forgot themselves for a moment, and called the Bahá'í Faith a religion. They slipped up here.

The seven members of the Local Spiritual Assembly just executed in Tabriz were:

> Mr Alláh-Virdí Mítháqí
> Mr Manúchihr Khádi'í
> Mr 'Abdu'l-'Alí Asadyárí
> Mr Ḥusayn Asadu'lláh-Zádih
> Mr Ismá'íl Zihtáb
> Dr Parvíz Fírúzí
> Mr Mihdí Báhirí

Killed with them in this second series of murders were their fellow Bahá'ís:

> Mr Ḥabíbu'lláh Taḥqíqí
> Dr Masrúr Dakhílí

This report went out immediately to over one-hundred-thousand centres in all parts of the world, as promised.

The entire Bahá'í world, and all their friends, were heart-stricken and shocked when they read the international publicity describing the 'ruthlessness and rapidity with which these precious lives of distinguished, virtuous members of the Bahá'í Community are being snuffed out, their honour violated, their homes and possessions plundered.'

No need to review the false charges made against these innocent, law-abiding, peace-loving, loyal citizens of an ungrateful country. They are the same fraudulent statements that have already brought world shame to Tabriz and Iran.

Improper trials, trumped-up charges, pre-arranged verdicts, every one of which proclaims to all the world:

'Bahá'ís in Iran must die!'

Numbered among the victims of this latest massacre in Tabriz were well-to-do doctors and engineers. They were well-dressed when they were illegally arrested and imprisoned. When their bodies were returned to their families for burial, they were dressed in shabby rags. The torturemongers of Iran steal from the living, and they steal from the dead. There is a name for those who rob the bodies of the departed.

They are called: *Ghouls*!

11

A Duet of Terror

1

'Good night, Harry!'

I was awakened in the middle of the night by a telephone call from a friend. He was not a Bahá'í, but he was very upset. He wanted to know what was happening in Iran.

He had just read in the *Los Angeles Times* about the execution of several Bahá'ís in Teheran. Earlier, he had watched a television program in which a Government official from Iran had repeated the same old charges against the Bahá'í Faith with which you are all too familiar by this time.

Harry was outraged.

'How *dare* they say such terrible things about the Faith?'

'We've been trying to answer the charges whenever we get the chance, Harry.'

'Well, you're not doing a good job! Not by half! I'd never even heard some of the wretched things this fellow was saying about the Bahá'í Faith.'

'Of course, you hadn't, Harry. None of them are true.'

'All lies?'

'Every single one. Without exception. False and baseless.'

'Then why isn't some Bahá'í answering these beggars?'

'We *are*, Harry. Every chance we get.'

'You'd better arrange a few more chances, and bring up

133

your big guns. This fellow was pretty convincing. He even had me worried.'

'You should know better, Harry. You should have been a Bahá'í yourself, years ago.'

'I *know*. I'm a slow starter. You know that, Bill. But I'll tell you one thing, if the rest of these Iranian officials are as smooth as this joker, you Bahá'ís are in for some real trouble.'

'We know that, Harry. We're already in it. We have been for nearly one hundred and fifty years.'

'Yeah, but I'm talking *right now,* this very minute stuff. If he can get me to wondering and boiling over, how about some poor soul who doesn't know anything at all about the Bahá'í Faith? He'll be a pushover for all that oil.'

'We're trying to prevent it, Harry.'

'I think you're taking it too lightly. Even the people in my office are beginning to ask questions.'

'That's exactly what they want, Harry. To sow the seeds of doubt.'

'Well, they're doing a good job. Better than you.'

'Truth will win out in the long run, Harry.'

'I'm worried about the short run. I really wanted to hit this guy.'

'You've got the wrong spirit, Harry.'

'Maybe so, but just this morning, my boss said that maybe there's a kernel of truth behind all these rumours and charges against the Bahá'í Faith.'

'There isn't, Harry. Not an ounce. Nobody knows that better than you.'

'Then get on the television and radio and blast these wretches. Stomp on 'em! Otherwise people are going to say "Where there's smoke, there's fire." Right?'

'They'd be absolutely right, Harry.'

'What do you mean, right?'

'In this case the old saying is true. "Where there's

smoke, there's fire." But not the version the present regime in Iran is trying to peddle.'

'I don't follow.'

'The smoke, Harry, is from the burning of more than a thousand Bahá'í homes in Iran.'

'Are you kidding?'

'I'm deadly serious. Over three hundred houses in Shiraz alone.'

'Then why aren't you telling the world about it? That's simply terrible!'

'We are, Harry. You've just been living in your cocoon again. Chances are some innocent Bahá'í's home is going up in smoke right now while we're talking.'

'I hate it!'

'We all do.'

'Get after them!'

'We're trying, Harry. They murdered a friend of mine and his son. I won't forget that.'

'Where did that happen?'

'In a town named Miyan-Du'ab. My wife, Marguerite, and I have been there together, as guests of the Local Assembly at the Bahá'í Centre. These terrorists burned that Centre to the ground, Harry. And eighty other houses in the region along with it. That's your smoke. They confiscate the homes, loot them, sell the furniture, and put a match to the people's houses while they look on, helpless to prevent it.'

'That's got to be illegal. Why don't the authorities do something about it?'

'They did, Harry. They set the fires.'

'I'm not prepared to believe *that*.'

'You'd better, Harry. It's a matter of public record in the newsrooms the world over, not to mention the United Nations. Their terrorists have burned houses from the Caspian Sea to the Gulf of Oman, from Iraq to Afghanistan. No place is safe.'

'Is that a fact?'

'Fact.'

'Really?'

'Really. I've got the cablegram about Miyan-Du'ab right here on the desk in front of me, Harry. BAHA'I CENTRE DESTROYED IN MIYAN-DU'AB. FATHER AND SON MURDERED.'

'But why, Bill? *Why?*'

'They were Bahá'ís.'

'That's no reason. That's criminal.'

'Isn't it though?'

'My blood is beginning to boil.'

'Turn up the heat, Harry, and you may catch up with me.'

'You said something about the *fire?*'

'I did indeed. These assassins and terrorists, not content with burning down the Centre in Miyan-Du'ab and killing the caretaker and his son, incited an enraged mob to drag their bodies through the streets. They carved those two dear souls to pieces with knives, and threw their dismembered parts into the flames of a bonfire they had kindled for that very purpose. That's your fire, Harry. Is it good enough?'

'That's absolutely the most awful thing I ever heard.'

'These persecutions are happening every day to the Bahá'ís in Iran, Harry. No one is safe. Sometimes it's even worse than in Miyan-Du'ab.'

Harry was livid. He shouted at me.

'Then why aren't you personally *doing* something about it? Instead of sitting around talking? Why don't you go on television and denounce these murderers? Or radio? Or take out full page ads in the papers? Anything! Write a book about it!'

'Good night, Harry.'

2

A Hero's Welcome!

Asadu'lláh Mukhtárí left his home in Birjand one morning, driving his flock of sheep before him. It was a sunny, cheerful day. In the evening, the sheep came home alone. Asadu'lláh was found the next day in the fields near his home. He had been stoned to death.

Asadu'lláh Mukhtárí was martyred on a Monday morning.

Asadu'lláh and his family had often suffered before at the hands of the people of their neighbourhood. After all, the Mukhtárís were Bahá'ís and the neighbours were hostile. Asadu'lláh had been beaten with clubs, pounded with fists, and struck on the head with heavy stones. Twice he had been bedridden for months. His head was crushed, his body bruised and scarred.

Everyone, especially his neighbours, expected Asadu'-lláh Mukhtárí to die. He refused to die. In spite of pain and difficulty Asadu'lláh was up once again, as soon as possible, tending his sheep.

On two separate occasions Asadu'lláh's home had been looted of all its furniture. It always happened when the old shepherd and his family were away. They were very poor. It would be a long time before they would be able to save enough money to buy any kind of furniture again.

Fortunately, he still had his sheep.

Then, one day, while Asadu'lláh and his wife and children were away from home visiting their family and friends in another village, someone stole his small flock of sheep.

It was all Asadu'lláh had in this world to support his family. He knew very well that the sheep had been stolen and driven off by their neighbours. Being completely fearless, he went to the neighbours to recover them.

To his great sorrow, Asadu'lláh found that his entire

flock had already been slaughtered. The meat and profits had been divided among the thieves.

He reminded the criminals that, according to their own religion and Holy Book, they were not permitted to eat stolen food.

They laughed, and replied:

'Our ulama (priests) tell us that it is not a crime to steal the property of Bahá'ís. It is praise to God. Worship. We will be rewarded by both God and man whenever we take and dispose of what belongs to the Bahá'ís.' 'Everybody in Iran knows that.'

They laughed at Asadu'lláh's helplessness.

On another occasion a mob of more than a hundred strong besieged Asadu'lláh's tiny home. Again they carried off the few possessions he had gradually acquired since their last theft. Before leaving, laden with Asadu'-lláh's property, they took time to torture the old shepherd a bit. They tried once again to force him to recant his belief in Bahá'u'lláh and the Bahá'í Faith.

'Deny your faith!' they insisted.

Asadu'lláh shook his head. To himself he said, 'Will they never learn?'

His steadfast refusal, in the face of direct threats, made the mob all the more angry. One of them suggested, 'Let's cut his throat.' Others favoured burning the old shepherd alive.

Asadu'lláh Mukhtárí was calm and serene through it all. Fearlessly, he said to them: 'I have some excellent logs in my storage bin, and a container of kerosene.'

He took a box of matches from his pocket and handed it to the ringleader. 'Here,' he said. 'Do as you please. I am at your mercy.'

The crowd hesitated. Asadu'lláh's bravery and contempt for their threats had shamed them. The old shepherd, firm as a rock, declared: 'Even if you burn me alive, I am still a Bahá'í. I will never give up my Faith.'

His family moved solidly to his side.

Asadu'lláh announced, 'Even if you burn all of us because we are Bahá'ís, you will not hear a single word besides that from any of us. We are Bahá'ís. We will remain Bahá'ís.'

The bravery and fearlessness of Asadu'lláh and his family had a dampening effect even on the hatred of those stony-hearted criminals. A few of them started to leave, grumbling, unsatisfied, but inwardly shamed.

They left the house grudgingly. The ringleader brazenly warned Asadu'lláh that they would surely return another day.

They did.

This time they caught the old man alone in the fields with his sheep. They clubbed him to death holding stones in their fists.

A number of the murderers were defiant enough to attend the inquest into Asadu'lláh's death. They knew they would never be punished for killing a Bahá'í. After all, as was said on so many occasions, 'that's what Bahá'ís are for'.

It was surprising that they bothered to hold an inquest, but Asadu'lláh Mukhtárí, though only a solitary shepherd, was a well-known figure. He had friends as well as enemies.

The killers who attended the inquest boldly shouted throughout. They insisted that they didn't want this old shepherd's body buried in their town. They became quite violent about it.

'It would be sacrilegious,' they said, 'to have a Bahá'í body buried in a decent town.'

A decent town of murderers! They saw no irony in it.

During the inquest, they boasted openly that they were the ones who had killed the old man. With their bare hands. They had pounded him to death with stones and fists. They admitted it, and warned all the Bahá'ís present that their turn was coming soon. They would all be killed.

'Depend on it,' they threatened.

They warned the Bahá'ís that there would soon be trouble all over the country. The time had come, they insisted, for Bahá'ís to denounce their false religion and become Muslims. Or die. Soon, they would have no other choice. Any of them.

The Bahá'ís remained silent.

The police tried to quieten the ruffians. Not to protect the Bahá'ís, but to get on with the inquest. The killers didn't care. In front of the police, they even threw stones and pebbles at the Bahá'ís who were attending the inquest.

These self-confessed murderers were finally charged by the police. That itself was an unexpected victory for the Bahá'ís. The police felt obliged to do something. After all, there was no denying they were guilty. They had confessed to the crime themselves, publicly, openly. The police, although reluctant, had no choice but to detain them.

It was a hollow victory. Everyone knew that it was only a formality necessitated by the circumstances. After all, even the police had been amused when the criminals had so loudly claimed the murder as their own.

It is a way with terrorists these days all over the world to claim responsibility, even for horrible and shameful deeds.

Asadu'lláh had been killed for living the kind of life that both Muhammad and Bahá'u'lláh would have praised and admired.

Asadu'lláh Mukhtárí was a Bahá'í. He had died for it.

His murderers had broken every law of God and man. Yes, they were detained. But only temporarily. The inquiry was a mockery. The murderers were completely exonerated of any blame. All of them. They returned in triumph to their homes to the cheers and applause of their neighbours who gave them a hero's welcome.

12

Children

1

Hurrah for the ten-year-old Ayatollah!

We have written much about the courage, steadfastness and heroism of the adult Bahá'í martyrs, but we have heard very little about the children. They encounter hatred and prejudice daily and meet it with courage and devotion. Some of them are heroic. It is only fair to point out that the majority of the children, even at a tender age, are as courageous and steadfast as their parents.

The children and youth of Bahá'í families have always been in the forefront of the teaching work. They love to hear the stories about the Báb and Bahá'u'lláh, and repeat them to their companions.

The Báb in His writings foretold that the children of this new day would be quite different. The children of the magnificent Age which He was ushering in, He said, would be like the wise men of past ages. In His own words:

> The newly born babe of that Day excels the wisest and most venerable men of this time, and the lowliest and most unlearned of that period shall surpass in understanding the most erudite and accomplished divines of this age.

Thousands of Bahá'í children in these days face cruel afflictions in the schools of Iran.

Most of these children are very studious. They often are more knowledgeable than other children of their own age. To acquire knowledge so that they can be of more service to their fellow men, is an instruction of the Founder of their Faith, Bahá'u'lláh. They love Bahá'u'lláh with all their hearts. So they apply themselves to their studies. They want to become teachers and pioneers, and the very best at whatever profession they decide to follow.

Their Bahá'í teachings tell them that as they grow up, they must become 'distinguished' among the peoples of the world, outstanding in all their acts. The most important thing for them to remember is that they must become noble and spiritual human beings, of service to mankind.

The children try with all their hearts to be faithful to these instructions. They acquire knowledge.

In the classes at school, and in their Bahá'í homes, every day of their lives they learn the spirit of fellowship and love. Not only in words, but in deeds and action. They are taught that their whole life must be a good-natured, friendly, loving prayer of service and usefulness to all people, Bahá'í and non-Bahá'í alike.

They can never fulfil that goal unless they have a good education. Therefore, they work hard, enjoy their studies, and, as a result, are usually fine students.

Most of the Bahá'í children know their Islamic religious lessons better than their fellow students who are Muslim. They can read the Koran and interpret it better than their Muslim counterparts, sometimes even better than their teachers.

The teachers complain to the Bahá'í parents that, because of this, the Bahá'í children are sometimes made prayer leaders. They are nicknamed by their fellow students 'Ayatollahs' because of their deep understanding of the Koran.

This causes much trouble for the little ten-year-old Bahá'í 'Ayatollahs'.

2

Three against one! Ninety years against ten!

Bahá'í children with such understanding, knowledge and intelligence, are not favoured at all by the Ministry of Education. According to the Ministry, children should all be 'guided to the right path', which, in their minds, means to Islam.

The Bahá'í community in Iran is very much aware that the Ministry pursues a detailed and organized plan against the Bahá'í children in all the schools of Iran. There is ample evidence of it. It is an important part of the overall plan of the clergy to obliterate the Bahá'í community.

There could be no more touching and heroic drama to witness than these young ones standing firm and courageous in the face of their tormentors. Adults, three at a time, confronting one small but courageous Bahá'í child.

The bravery of these little Bahá'ís pleases the other children in their class. Not all are unfriendly. When these confrontations take place in the general classroom, many of the other children are sympathetic to the Bahá'ís. They remember the friendship and love which these Bahá'í children have always shown so generously and spontaneously.

No one responds more quickly or more sincerely to love than children. If left to themselves, they would never be prejudiced one against another because of religion, nor would their hearts be full of hate. It is only when poisonous thoughts are planted in their naturally innocent minds that they arise against their Bahá'í classmates.

Sometimes a confrontation between a teacher who may be thirty years old and a Bahá'í child of ten or eleven takes place before the entire class.

The teacher begins with a barrage of insults and false statements about the Bahá'í Faith. He harangues the child.

These Bahá'í children have courageous spirits, and do not quietly accept insults against their Faith. They resist them. Their protests against the injustice of the teacher touch off what amounts to a public discussion about the Bahá'í Faith in front of the class.

The unexpectedly impressive responses which that young child gives to the teacher's questions and comments often leave the teacher speechless. Expecting an easy victory, he finds instead that he has cornered a ten-year-old tiger.

It becomes like a game for the classroom. Like a tennis match: Attack, defend! Forehand, backhand! Volley, smash!

The children begin to respond to each one of the young Bahá'í's answers.

Question, answer. Applause.

Question, answer. Cheers.

Cries of 'Hurrah!'

'The Bahá'í has overcome the mighty instructor!'

The children in the class delight in it. The teacher, however, does not.

Frustrated by the answers the Bahá'í child gives, he becomes angrier and angrier. At last he leaves the classroom to consult with other teachers.

They come to his rescue.

They call for that same Bahá'í child at an hour when he has other classes, such as gymnastics or mathematics. They force him, against his wishes, to discuss the Bahá'í Faith with them. They are now three to one.

They argue and argue, shouting louder and louder, trying to wear him down. With one such child, their complete and frustrating failure, even at such odds, led to violence and a beating. This was followed by forcing that brave young boy to copy out dreadful passages from an insulting booklet which attacked his Faith.

The child was sickened and became ill. When the doctor was summoned, he said that his severe headaches were caused by the extreme pressure put upon such a young and tender mind and by the lies he was forced to write.

This is not an isolated instance. Similar things happen to these poor Bahá'í children day after day. Picture this. Three adult ideologists trained by the Ministry of Education are sent for. They, with a number of the older students, join forces to confront a Bahá'í child of ten or eleven. With all their power and shouting, they try to shatter the very foundation of this little fellow's beliefs. Hour after hour they will hold him as a captive audience, surrounded by enemies, a lamb encircled by wolves who close in on all sides.

They use every unfair tactic they can think of to frighten him and to refute whatever he says, or whatever he has been taught at home.

Picture this marvellous ending to all their attacks: they fail!

They are bewildered when they realize that all their efforts against one young boy have been in vain. They are in truth not only wonder-struck at the heroic steadfastness of this child, but are shaken inwardly by the remarkable replies which they have received to their insulting questions.

The Bahá'í children who have been taught to honour all the Messengers of God, which certainly includes Muhammad, reply with beautiful verses from the Koran which disprove and destroy the attack being made against them by their teachers. They support these quotations with similar texts they have memorized from the writings of their own Faith. They refuse to bend before the onslaught launched against them.

Sometimes it means a beating. Sometimes they are expelled from school for their belief in this 'false religion'. It often depends on how angered their teacher has become by his frustration.

On at least two occasions, students have been abducted

by these religious education teachers who have been so ignominiously defeated by the words of their own Holy Book, the Koran.

Girl students, against their wills, have been forcibly married to Muslims, and denied access to their parents.

3

'My father was killed because he was a Bahá'í.'

An instructor of religious education entered a classroom. His first question was: 'Is there anyone in this class who does not belong to the true religion?'

No one replied.

The instructor insisted.

'What I meant,' he said, 'is there a Bahá'í in this class?'

A fifteen-year-old girl stood up.

'I', she said, 'am a Bahá'í.'

The teacher in abusive and insulting language announced to the class:

'Let it be known to all of you that this girl is defiled and untouchable, and none of you are to have any contact with her.'

The teacher demanded that the Bahá'í girl go to the back of the room and sit at a desk by herself. He stated that this arrangement was to be observed to the end of the year; no one was allowed to sit next to a Bahá'í.

The children in a class in Yazd were asked to write an essay on what had happened to them during the summer.

The eleven-year-old daughter of one of the seven martyrs of Yazd wrote a sweet and factual essay about what had happened to her when the Revolutionary Guards came to their house and took her beloved father away to prison. She wrote of her visit to her father in that prison, recalled the moment when they had heard that her darling father had been shot to death as a martyr. Her essay was so moving, it brought tears to the eyes of the teacher and the children in her class.

However, since she had used the word 'Bahá'í' in the essay, the teacher, though moved, was also annoyed. The Bahá'í girl should have known better. The teacher took the essay to the headmistress.

The young girl was told, 'Your essay deserved to receive the highest marks, but since you mentioned the word "Bahá'í" a few times, your essay must be withdrawn.'

The girl replied: 'I was told to write about what had happened to me this summer. This all happened to me. Whatever I have written is the exact truth. My father was killed because he was a Bahá'í.'

In Zanjan, a city official seized one of the four sons of a Bahá'í family, and spread-eagled his body on the ground. The young boy had said that his heart was ablaze with the fire of his love for the Báb.

This illustrious leader of the city built a fire on that young lad's chest, so that his breast might really taste what it meant to be on 'fire'.

The boy had only to recant and he would be saved, he was told.

As the fire grew hotter and more fierce, and the pain more intense, he merely smiled at his persecutors, and said, 'Do you think you can terrorize or frighten me into being like you are?'

He died. The flames consumed his body through that breast in which beat a heart of love for the Báb and His Faith.

He could 'stand fast' because he *knew* what he was dying for.

It is on this rock of belief with which no treasure in life can compare, that the terrorists and Stone-Age torturers of Iran will finally break their teeth.

Younger and younger children are being put to the test.

The youngest was five. He was preparing himself in the kindergarten to be admitted into Grade 1 next year. He already knew six prayers by heart, and a number of extracts from the Bahá'í writings. He was quite an astonishing child. Well-behaved, intelligent, quick to learn, and he recited what he had learned very eloquently.

When the Inspector from the Ministry of Education came to the school, the teacher was eager to boast about how successful he had been in teaching these children in his class; so, naturally, he called on his prize pupil to recite the verses he had learned. His performance astonished and delighted the visiting Inspector. As a final effort, the teacher asked the boy to recite another poem, one which began with the sentence, 'I am a Muslim child.'

The little boy gazed silently at his teacher without uttering a word.

The teacher repeated his request. But the child still remained silent. The teacher was surprised, and became uneasy. He was embarrassed in front of the Inspector. He could not understand why the boy, who was so exceptional in learning and reciting poetry, should now remain silent.

The teacher asked the little boy, 'Why don't you recite the poem?'

The little boy said, 'Because I am *not* a Muslim child. I am a Bahá'í.'

The Inspector left the room in anger. He complained to the headmaster who summoned the boy's mother to the school. She was warned that this little boy should be instructed not to talk about the Bahá'í Faith to his classmates.

When the mother found out what had happened, she naturally told her five-year-old son that he should be wise and careful. The boy, who had learned in the Bahá'í community about being brave and steadfast, could not accept this. He replied to his mother: 'I *am* a Bahá'í and I will always tell people that I am, and if they bother me I will go to the nearest police station and complain.'

Poor little one! He was still to learn that for him, there *is* no police station.

But learn it he will, and be stronger than ever, this five-year-old spiritual child.

A Letter from Yazd

To conclude this chapter on the Bahá'í children of Iran, I can do no better than offer you the following extracts from a letter written from Yazd on November 3, 1981 – after this book had supposedly been completed. It tells the story simply, heroically, and far better than I ever could. The writer was herself arrested and imprisoned a few weeks later.

My dear Brother,

   ... I do not know where to begin, there is too much to be written about. In these days of constant struggle our children are in the vanguard. They always produce wonders. What is transpiring here is exceptional. Where were these heroes before? They must have existed but it is only now that they are able to manifest their spiritual potentialities, to reveal their precious essence, to prove the validity of the spiritual training they received from their families.

Most of our children, in different degrees, have now been given opportunities in their schools to demonstrate their heroism. In the Land of Ya [Yazd], the home of the brave, opportunities abound. So far, over 100 of our children have been expelled from their schools because they are Bahá'ís. Their dismissals, which ordinarily one would expect would be the cause of sadness, have produced in them a joy and vitality which I cannot describe. Because of their response to their dismissals, all Yazd is shaken. Our precious children have shown such courage as to have caused all

Yazd to wonder. It should be said that all these children are among the very best students in the city. They attained the highest marks, were known for their exemplary conduct and were recognized as being exceptionally talented and intelligent. This has given rise to the first question among the people of Yazd: 'Why should the best be expelled?'

The second question in the minds of those who have expelled them arises from the courage and perseverance of these young ones. Although they were dismissed from school in an atmosphere charged with hatred and prejudice, our children have, with a sense of pride and a consciousness of being related to the followers of Bahá'u'lláh, collected their books and school-bags with placid joy and left the school, smiling and walking with a light step, while their non-Bahá'í school friends wept for them.

I have to interrupt this letter as the telephone is ringing.

(*Later*)

I have been informed that six members of the Local Spiritual Assembly of Teheran have been arrested. Never a dull moment! What strength is required to be able to concentrate our thoughts and compose our feelings!

I was writing about our children. The believers of Yazd have told us that there are very few Bahá'í children in the city who are unhappy and cry – they are those who as yet have not been expelled from the schools.

The teachers, and even headmasters, are extremely upset by the instruction from the Ministry to dismiss Bahá'í children. One headmaster decided to resign after receiving the order to dismiss his Bahá'í students, but he was firmly warned against tendering his resignation. However, on the day of the dismissal of the Bahá'í students he absented himself from school, having clearly stated that he had no wish to witness such an unjust action.

(*Later*)

I have been interrupted by another phone call. A husband and wife in Karaj have been executed by firing-squad for their 'Zionist' activities. My thoughts immediately go out to Mr and Mrs — who are imprisoned in Karaj. Is this news true? Is it about them? Until we can verify this report, what anxiety we have to endure! The air is thick with rumours these days, none of them good. God knows what consternation fills our minds until we are able to verify the truth or falsehood of these rumours.

I'm sorry... I was diverted again. This is what is happening to our children:

On the appointed day the teacher asks the class whether there are any Bahá'ís among the students. Our children – our patient, well-behaved, faithful and steadfast children – stand up and with great pride and courage introduce themselves as Bahá'ís. They are then sent to the office of the headmaster. The teachers, and sometimes the headmasters, are embarrassed and sad. In the office of the headmaster the children are first asked to deny their faith and continue their studies. These requests are in many instances expressed with love and concern, because the staff in the school really like these distinguished and outstanding students and do not want to lose them. But what they hear from these children surprises them. The children announce that they are Bahá'ís, that they personally decided to be Bahá'ís, that they cannot lie and deny their faith, and that they are proud of what they believe! At this point the headmaster and teachers have no alternative but to sign the order expelling them.

These children range in age from 7 to 17 or 18. It is a

sight to see how cheerfully the Bahá'í children leave the school with no sense of shame, while their non-Bahá'í fellow students look on thoughtfully, some even weeping. Disturbances occur in the classroom after the Bahá'í children leave, and challenging discussion takes place between the remaining pupils and their teachers. The children put questions until the end of the school day and the discussion is carried out to the streets. The non-Bahá'í students invariably ask: 'Isn't it true that we are supposed to have freedom of belief? What's wrong with the Bahá'í children – don't they worship God and pray? Why are they being dismissed?' The children carry their questions home. Their queries spread to all parts of the city and are taken up in the streets and the bazaars.

The parents of the dismissed Bahá'í children – themselves the essence of patience and steadfastness – exclaim with pride: 'What we have failed to achieve, our children are now achieving!' They praise the children with candour and love. I doubt whether in the history of any society such honour has been heaped upon children of so tender an age. The parents remark: 'It is true that in the 138 years since the beginning of our Faith we have endured many hardships, but we have never been so successful as our children in proclaiming to the masses of the people of Yazd the exalted character of the Bahá'í Revelation, nor have our actions resulted, as have our children's, in creating an atmosphere in which the Faith is being discussed so openly among the people in the streets and bazaars. Our persecuted children have succeeded in breaking through the barrier of prejudice of the hard-hearted people of this city.'

The parents go on to exclaim: 'The events of the past have made us conservative and cautious; it is our children who have changed the atmosphere.' ... This change had its early beginnings last year when the martyrs shed their blood on the soil of Yazd. This change cannot be measured by existing standards.

A programme of study has been arranged for our children at home; they are learning with great speed and progressing in all fields of knowledge. They will surely surpass their fellow students who are still in school. More important than this, we have promised ourselves to help these children become so well versed in the holy writings that each will become the envy of scholars. There is no doubt that this will come to pass.

Let me tell you something about the adults. The Bahá'í men and women – particularly the women – are facing tribulations with such equanimity that no comparable example can be found even among the legendary heroines of the past. These women are in fact creating new legends through their patience, steadfastness, love and detachment. They have conquered the hearts of everyone and won the praises of all. The forces of hatred have been vanquished by the power of their faith. When they are looted of their property, furniture and belongings, they part with them as they would with outworn dolls and playthings, looking on as though they were mere spectators. They shower love upon those who come to take away their belongings as might an affectionate and indulgent parent who with a smile will give a worthless toy or plaything to a naughty child. It appears that they even enjoy the naughtiness of these children.

Such behaviour has greatly influenced the hearts of the looters who are not great in number. Mr K – that heartless man who is the leader of those who are executing the Bahá'ís and confiscating their properties, and whose main task is to uproot the Faith in Yazd – is often seen entering the homes of the Bahá'ís, knocking upon their doors at any hour of the day or night. He has become such a familiar figure that the Bahá'ís jest with him, saying, 'You have become one of us!' He even knows the nicknames of the Bahá'í children. If he does not make an appearance for some time the Bahá'ís tell him they miss him. Although Mr K comes to take away their property or to send their loved ones to prison, they are pleasant to him, joke with him, inquire about his health. They even tell him that one day he should become a Bahá'í in order to understand the significance of what he is now doing.

... The Bahá'ís of Yazd say that this unfeeling man, Mr K, is treated by them as a member of the family. When he comes to seize their furniture the young men of the family help him carry out the heavier pieces; when he arrives they invite him to join them at the table and give him sweets, fruits, even meals. After he has eaten he goes around the house and selects the furniture he wants to take away. If he does not have a vehicle available he gestures toward the selected articles of furniture and tells the owner, 'These are my trust with you; keep them safely until I return.' He sometimes even proposes that the family might buy back the furniture from him! The behaviour of the long-suffering Bahá'ís in these appalling circumstances is unprecedented. They recognize that they are indeed giving away worthless dolls, as to an ignorant child.

The Bahá'ís whose homes have been confiscated do not leave the city but move to a small dwelling place, wherever they can find refuge ... Almost all the Bahá'í men have been required to leave the city and this has provided the children, youth, and women an opportunity to prove their courage and valour. How proud we are of them! What a creation has Bahá'u'lláh raised up! Such conduct has been unheard of, even in legends. When the Bahá'ís of Yazd themselves relate these events they express amazement at the change in themselves. The people of Yazd have the reputation of being economical and thrifty; it is said that two families of Yazd could fight between themselves over possession of a valueless stick of wood. But look at them now! They have given up everything to show their love for Bahá'u'lláh. When one extends sympathy to them they express surprise, remarking that what they have parted with is worthless. They do not even denounce the thieves and looters when referring to them.

I cannot overlook mentioning a mother and daughter who are in prison – they are examples. The daughter is 60 years old and the mother is over 80. The fact of imprisoning such elderly innocent women is in itself very strange, but it has been done. These women are Bahá'ís of Zoroastrian background. All their possessions were confiscated and they are now in the women's prison with over 100 prisoners of all kinds.

A few months ago a release order was issued for the mother, but she refused to leave unless her daughter was also released; so they remained in prison. Only ten days ago the authorities at last gave permission for them to receive occasional visitors.

Bahá'í visitors have witnessed the old woman embracing and demonstrating affection to the police-woman, before she would come forward to meet her visitors. During the course of the visit the old woman noticed a young male guard who was supposed to control the visitors. In her special Parsi-Yazdi accent she maternally addressed complimentary remarks to him with such obvious love and sincerity that the young man was visibly uncomfortable and ashamed. She remarked to her visitors, 'I always thought that mothers could really love only their own children, but I have come to feel genuine love for these young men who are on duty.' The young guard had nothing to say, but stood with bowed head.

The fire of sincere love is melting the ice of hatred. Then with remarkable candour this old woman, more than 80 years of age, said to her visitors, 'Tell everybody that Bahá'u'lláh has enabled me to perform miracles. Tell them that the Bahá'í prayers which I copy out for the sick ones in this prison cause them to become cured.' She related how one of the guards sought her out excitedly to tell her his story. 'I was searching for you,' he said. 'I wanted to tell you that the prayers you wrote out for me and my wife a year ago have been answered and our wish to have a baby is fulfilled. This has made it unnecessary for me to divorce my wife for her inability to conceive a child.'

In the evenings the women prisoners crowd together around the mother and daughter and ask them to tell them stories and speak to them. They speak most beautifully and with such a sweet accent that nobody wants to go to sleep. Even the guards do not object.

When Sarafráz, the mother, has a visitor, she begs them to bring fruit from her orchard in order to make a feast for the prisoners. The old woman does not know that her orchard and other properties have been confiscated. But the visitors know what to do. They purchase large quantities of fruit so she can provide hospitality to her fellow prisoners. Where have you heard stories like this?

Glad tidings! Glad tidings! The climate of this city in the midst of the desert is changed and the perfume of the love of God has filled all corners. In my next letter I will write you more such stories – if I am still alive, or free . . .

13

The Banner of Islam

1

The Mirrors of God

If anyone wants to know exactly how a Bahá'í feels about Islam and Muhammad, there is a very simple direct way to show this. It cannot be misunderstood and it cannot be misrepresented.

You will see this from the drawing on the next page. It is based upon the words of Bahá'u'lláh in His *Book of Certitude*, written to bring about an understanding and appreciation of the oneness of all religions.

This one drawing alone should banish forever any mistaken ideas any sincere Muslim might have about the love and respect each Bahá'í, without exception, feels for Islam, its Prophet, and its Holy Book.

The drawing indicates only *four* of the great Messengers of God. For the sake of simplicity and brevity, we have mentioned only Moses, Christ, Muhammad and Bahá'u'lláh, but it is equally true for *all* God's Messengers. The drawing should, of course, include the Founders of all the great revealed religions: Moses, Krishna, Zoroaster, Buddha, Christ, Muhammad, the Báb, Bahá'u'lláh – all the great Messengers of God without exception.

Since Bahá'ís love Bahá'u'lláh, they must clearly love Muhammad as well. The drawing leaves no doubt. If they *do not* love Muhammad, they just as clearly do not love Bahá'u'lláh.

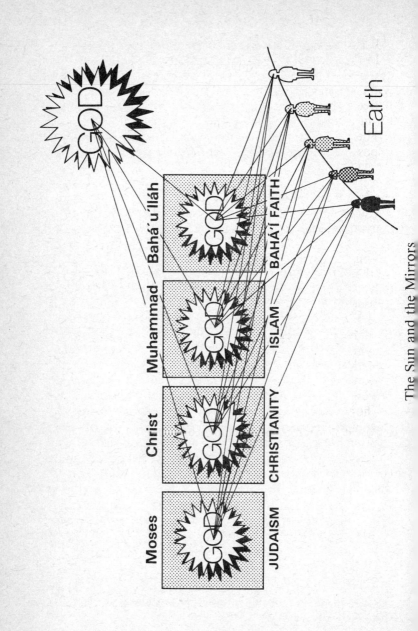

The Sun and the Mirrors

It is that simple, that true, and that obvious.

In reality, if they lack this same unquestioned love for any one of these great Messengers of God, they are not Bahá'ís at all. There would be no need for their persecutors to try to make them say: 'We are not Bahá'ís', for in truth, they would not be.

The drawing also shows clearly why it is both impossible and unthinkable for Bahá'ís to bend before the cruel torture and persecutions besetting them in Iran, and agree to give up the Bahá'í Faith and become Muslims. It shows unmistakably how foolish such a demand really is. By such a recantation, they would be living a lie, and denying everything that Muhammad Himself stood for. They would be denying the entire Plan of God for man.

Thus, you can see why the Bahá'ís in Iran refuse to give up their belief in Bahá'u'lláh. To do so would mean that they would have to give up their belief in *all* God's Messengers. In truth, it would mean giving up belief in God Himself, the *Sun* which shines in all these Mirrors. By denying the Sunlight in one Mirror, they would be denying the Sun.

Nothing could be plainer than this.

How beautiful and exciting the Oneness of God and all his religions becomes when the truth is once made known.

These, of course, are not *my* explanations. They are from the Founder of the Bahá'í Faith, Bahá'u'lláh.

One of the most important things the Promised One of all religions would do in the last days, would be to 'unseal the meaning of the Holy Books' and make them understandable to all mankind.*

* Bahá'u'lláh's *Book of Certitude (Kitáb-i-Íqán)* does exactly this. It answers those questions which have for so long troubled and divided religions, questions concerning Reincarnation, the story of Creation, Adam and Eve, Good and Evil, Heaven and Hell, the Trinity, the Eucharist, Confession, the Day of Judgment, the End of the world, and dozens more. It is the Book described by the prophet Daniel which would break 'the seals' of those 'words' destined to remain 'closed up' until the 'time of the end'. It answers with beauty and clarity all the problems that have separated the religions of the world. It has been called a 'matchless utterance'.

2

The Oneness of Religions

Let us look more closely at the proof of the oneness of all religions as given in that one simple drawing.

God is like the sun. The sun brings physical light to the world. Without that sunlight, everything on earth would perish.

God is the *spiritual Sun.* He brings spiritual Light to men's hearts. Without that special Light, men would perish spiritually.

The Messengers of God are like *Pure Mirrors.* They reflect God's Light upon all humanity, upon the entire world. The five little human figures in the drawing represent symbolically the five races of mankind.

The *physical sun* does not come down to earth, it sends its rays. In like manner, the *spiritual Sun,* God, does not come down to earth. He sends His Messengers, these Pure Mirrors of His perfections and virtues. *They* are the *Rays* of His Sun of Truth.

These Messengers of God, these Pure Mirrors, are the Light and Guidance of the entire world. Just as the rays of the physical sun sustain and develop all physical life on the planet, in like manner, the Spiritual Rays of the Spiritual Sun sustain and develop all *spiritual life* in the human race.

The physical sun doesn't appear once and never again. It rises and sets numberless times, and each of its appearances is called by a different name and continues the work it did before. Sunday, Monday, Tuesday; April, May, June; Spring, Summer, Autumn. *It is always the same sun.*

The spiritual Sun appears to men in like manner. It shines forth from a different Mirror, called by a different name: Moses, Jesus, Muhammad, Krishna, Buddha, the Báb, Bahá'u'lláh. *It is always the same Sun.*

Nothing could be plainer once we have seen the answer

given to us by Bahá'u'lláh in His explanation of the Suns and the Mirrors.

The answers which Bahá'u'lláh has given to the other puzzling questions that have divided and separated the religions of the world are equally clear and self-evident.

3

That love will never alter

Now look at the second drawing (p. 162). It is a close-up of one section of the more detailed drawing shown earlier. It will concentrate our understanding even more clearly on the fundamental love and reverence that fills every Bahá'í heart the world over in its remembrance of Bahá'u'lláh, Founder of the Bahá'í Faith, and Muhammad, Founder of Islam.

This drawing could just as easily be the Mirrors of *Christ and Bahá'u'lláh, Moses and Bahá'u'lláh, Buddha and Bahá'u'lláh*, or for that matter *Moses and Christ,* etc., for the basic principle holds true of all the great Messengers of God, and Their relationship to each other and to God.

They all share the same true *Sunlight of God* and reflect through Their teachings that same *Sunlight of Truth* upon the same mankind.

Each One of these *Mirrors,* Messengers of God, is closely and inseparably linked to each other Messenger of God, since They are *all* part of His one great redemptive scheme for mankind.

The love which every Bahá'í has for Muhammad, Moses, Buddha, Christ – all these great Spiritual World Educators of humanity – is not just a casual love, respect, and affection such as we have for an admired but distant friend or relative. It is a soul-inspiring, heart-warming love which is touched by the fire of God's inspiration. As the drawing shows, this love is in reality love for God, *through* His Messenger. Therefore, it is a deep-seated,

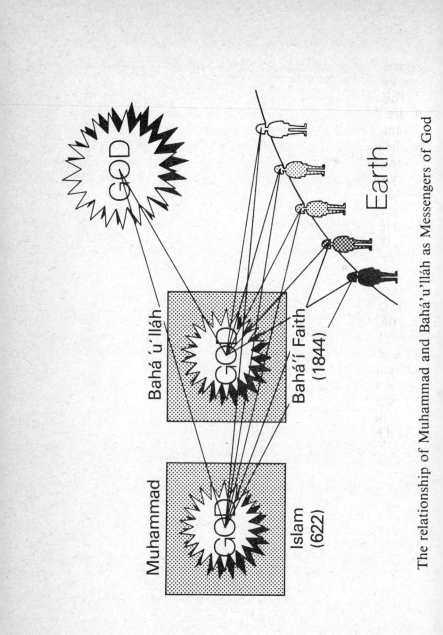

The relationship of Muhammad and Bahá'u'lláh as Messengers of God

sacred reverence, a consecrated devotion to *every* Messenger, every Mirror of God's Light and Truth.

This love, once understood, creates eagerness and desire to serve Him. It generates a desire to *teach* which inflamed the Apostles of Christ and set ablaze the hearts of the followers of all religions. It made them eager to share the wonder and excitement of eternal truth with everyone they met. It is this feeling of being 'on fire' with the love of God that has sent Bahá'í pioneers and teachers to over one hundred thousand places in the world.

So inspiring, so soul-uplifting, and all-consuming is this love, that the early believers in every great Messenger and Mirror of God are prepared to give their lives if necessary, for this wonderful, universal, thrilling belief. They have done so in the past. They are doing so today in Iran.

To deny Muhammad, or *any* Messenger of God, or to belittle Him, His Book, or His Religion would be unthinkable to a Bahá'í. It would be the same as denying Bahá'u'lláh. It would be betraying some of the most fundamental of all Bahá'í principles:

The *Oneness of God,* the *Oneness of Religion,* and the *Oneness of all His Messengers.*

To be an enemy of Islam and Muhammad, a Bahá'í would have to be an enemy of Bahá'u'lláh and the Bahá'í Faith, an enemy of every religion on the face of the earth. In fact, an enemy of God Himself and of His Holy Word.

Impossible!

You can see in one glance at the drawings of those Mirrors and the Sun, why the Bahá'ís in Iran could *never* entertain such an idea as a denial of their Faith. It would mean disgracing and dishonouring not only their own Messenger of God, Bahá'u'lláh, but Muhammad and all God's Messengers as well.

The Bahá'ís' love for Bahá'u'lláh and Muhammad and *every* Messenger of God will never alter and will never fade. You can see the reason why. You can also see why they feel honoured to be chosen to die for their Faith. We realize, at last, that they are not fanatical in their belief at all. They are logical and clear in the actions they take, consumed by a deep, abiding love for God and His Messengers.

When the persecutors in Iran fail to make a Bahá'í recant and say, 'I am *not* a Bahá'í', and kill him for his refusal, that Bahá'í becomes a special, unique and wonderful *new breed* of martyr.

He or she is dying not only for Bahá'u'lláh, but for Muhammad as well. Those martyrs in Iran today are dying, as the Suns and Mirrors tell us, for every Messenger of God and for every religion, including *yours*.

How foolish the charge now appears that the Bahá'í Faith could ever be an enemy of Islam. Although our story of 'The Banner of Islam' has hardly begun, we can already safely say:

Mark the charge: Refuted.

4

They are identical!

The refutation is devastatingly clear.

It so completely, and so thoroughly, demolishes those 'false charges' against my Bahá'í brothers and sisters in Iran, that I am tempted, because of the slang-nature of my profession as a sportscaster, as well as my feeling of pure joy, to say to the present regime in Iran:

'Play *that* on your piano!'

I know! The subject is far too serious and too dreadful to be flippant about. I *did* promise you that the false charges would not only be refuted, but would be demolished, so perhaps you can forgive my enthusiasm.

Let us continue with the demolition of this most false of all the accusations made against the Bahá'í Faith, for this *fraudulent charge,* 'enemy of Islam', lies at the heart of almost all the attacks.

Look once again at the original drawing. No, better

still, this time go outside into the real sunlight and do it yourself, *live.*

Humour me. Try it. Please.

All you need are two mirrors and a few minutes of your time. The rewards may be eternal. Ready?

All right. Now hold up the two mirrors, one in each hand. Let the sunlight reflect in each mirror as you look at them.

Now, over one mirror write: Muhammad. Over the second mirror, write: Bahá'u'lláh. It will be easier, of course, if you have a friend to hold up the two mirrors for you. I promise you both that it will be worth the trouble.

Have your friend hold up the two mirrors so that you can seen the sun reflected in each mirror at the same time.

Now you have *three* suns. One in each mirror, and the third and *real* sun still in the heavens. The suns in the two mirrors are a reflection of that real sun in the sky.

That's the way it is with God and His religion.

God (the Sun) remains alone in the heavens. Single, alone, unknowable, unfathomable, beyond our definition and description. Even to use the word *He* in connection with this great primal Force and Power borders on the sacrilegious, but we are obliged to use words to convey our thoughts, however inadequate or inexact.

Still, it is essential that we understand that God is infinite, and incomprehensible to finite man.

Even so, just as we know the physical sun by its rays, we know the Unknowable God by His Mirrors, His Messengers, by the Light, the virtues, the attributes and qualities which we see reflected to us on this earthly plane by these Pure Mirrors.

They are His (God's) Rays of Truth.

We are now outside once again, looking at these two mirrors with the sunlight reflected in each one.

Now, you tell me, while you are looking at those two identical mirrors, with the same sun shining in each one of them, which mirror do you think is better? Which is greater? Which mirror has more light? Which is more beautiful? Which sunlight do you prefer? Which do you love more? The mirror with the sunlight named Bahá'u'-lláh? Or the mirror with the sunlight of Muhammad?

Of course! They're identical.

You have to love them equally. How could you do otherwise? There is no difference between them whatsoever.

In order to be practical, and to carry out the work of God in every age, and to use the Sunlight which we are given when *our* Messenger of God comes, we not only give our love and allegiance to that Mirror, that Messenger of God Who appears in our time, we also arise and serve Him with all our hearts.

We have no other choice. It is the Light and Truth for that time in history.

We are ready to die for Him and His Truth, and His followers have done so in every age. Every martyr in his day was unique, and a *new breed* of martyr, and had nothing in common with those being killed in that same age by the violence of the world around them.

So it is in Iran today, and it is of significance and importance to all of us.

We use and need the sunlight of Friday, Saturday or Sunday because it is the only light available to us on those days. But Friday people do not hate or refuse to recognize the sunlight of Saturday when it comes, or they would be living forever on Friday. Nor do Saturday people refuse to accept the sunlight of Sunday when Saturday has gone.

You *know* the sun will come up again on Sunday, but if you reject it, or fail to recognize it, or to take advantage of its light and heat and life-giving power, you will be in the darkness of a day that has passed.

You will thus be deprived of all future light and life and hope. You will be missing the Sunlight of the new Day, the Source of all the spiritual survival on the planet in that Day. It has *always* been so in this great, progressive, religious scheme of God for man.

This is what *Prophecy* and the *Holy Books* are all about. Each Scripture has foretold the One that would come in the future with the new Day of God.

Therefore, if we accept Friday but deny Saturday, or accept Saturday but deny Sunday, it is very clear that we have given our allegiance to the name on the Mirror, and *not* to the Light that shines within it. We have remembered the Messenger, but have forgotten His Message and His Promise.

No mistake could be more tragic for mankind!

Now you know what has happened to the fanatics in Iran. They have drawn a curtain across the Face of God!

If they kill because of it, it is fanaticism. It has nothing whatsoever to do with the 'falseness' of the ones they are killing. It has only to do with their own ignorance of the great Day in which they are living.

It is not the Bahá'í community of Iran that is the enemy of Islam!

5

It is not the last!

Just as the charge that the Bahá'ís are enemies of Islam is at the heart of all the false charges, baseless accusations, and fraudulent misrepresentations made in Iran against the Bahá'í Faith, in like manner this episode, 'The Banner of Islam' is at the heart of *all* the refutation.

Therefore, so that the idea will be forever imprinted in our minds, that no people on earth have more love and respect for Muhammad and Islam than the Bahá'ís all over the world, (including Iran), let it be known:

In every Bahá'í House of Worship, in every continent, the words of Muhammad and the Koran are honoured and revered, together with the teachings of Moses, Christ, Buddha, and the Founders of all the great religions.

Not only is the Bahá'í Faith *not* an enemy of Islam and its Prophet, Muhammad, but Bahá'ís are among His greatest supporters, and have raised the glory of His Name in every part of the world. They have honoured and praised the Apostle of God, as they have honoured and praised the Messenger of every great Religion of God.

One of the most important and significant things that Bahá'u'lláh and the Bahá'í Faith have done for *all* religions, is to make it clear that religion itself is progressive and continuous, always unfolding a greater measure of truth in every age.

No religion is exclusive and final.

There is no exclusive salvation for the Jew, the Christian, the Buddhist, the Muslim, the Bahá'í, or for any single religion. God is not in competition with Himself.

For the first time in the history of religion, the teachers of the Bahá'í Faith make it clear that their own religion is *not* the last outpouring of Truth from God. Neither their religion nor their Messenger is the last and final Word of Truth which God will shower upon mankind.

This is a refreshing and exciting concept in religion.

Bahá'u'lláh's words prevent this dreadful scourge of exclusivity and finality from ever entering into religion again.

As mankind progresses, and his spiritual and material guidance stand in need of further outpouring of truth from that same Life-Giving Source – God, at such a time in history another Mirror, another Messenger of God will appear. He will bring the same One Light and Power from God, but His Message will be adapted and fitted to the needs of the Day in which He appears.

It is the Age and the Day in which a Messenger of God appears that is different, not the Messenger Himself. They are all One and the same.

While it is true that we are entering the Day of the

coming of age of humanity, the Day of the One Fold and One Shepherd, the time of the end, the last days, the Day of the eagerly-expected, long-awaited Christ-promised Kingdom of God on earth – while all this is true, it still does not mean, in spite of the majesty and glory of this present Age, that progressive revelation has ended, or that the continuous outpouring of Truth from God through His Messengers is over.

Never!

It is not the end, but in reality only the beginning. The most wonderful and exciting part lies ahead. The *Prophetic Cycle* leading up to this wondrous Day, a Day promised in every sacred Scripture of every great past religion, has ended. The *Cycle of Fulfilment* has begun.

This is that wondrous Day that *every* Prophet has talked about. It has come at last, in our time. It is here! It has begun! And people are dying for it in Iran.

We, and all the world, should be overjoyed and thrilled that it finally *has* come and is being started on its way.

It was in that room in His House in Shiraz that the Báb announced this wondrous Day, releasing thereby a new and wonderful 'spiritual force' into the world. From this we can begin to understand what a calamitous tragedy and terrible crime it was against *all* society, not just against the Bahá'í community in Iran, when that Holy House, that symbol of hope for the peoples of all nations, races and religions and for generations as yet unborn, was destroyed.

We also know why it will be restored to stand again in all its glory and beauty, no matter what the enemies of the Bahá'í Faith in Iran may do, either now or in the future. This is yet another reason why those Bahá'ís who are dying today in Iran are a *new breed* of martyrs. They are giving their lives for all mankind, and for its future, willingly, enthusiastically and courageously.

Hats off!

Another marvellous thing can be seen from that

drawing. The *Sun* and the *Mirrors of God* will go on forever. The Bahá'í Faith is not final, not exclusive, not the last stage of this grand redemptive scheme of God for man. It is *not* the last! The Bahá'í Faith is the Message, and Bahá'u'lláh is the Messenger, for *this* Day in the affairs of mankind. Not forever.

Bahá'u'lláh has brought the Laws, the Teachings, the Institutions, and above all, the Spirit, to establish and maintain a lasting peace among nations. He has come to raise up that world civilization which all mankind has long awaited and eagerly anticipated, the 'Christ-promised Kingdom of God on earth'.

The Bahá'í Faith accepts the Divine origin and inspiration of all those great religions of the past, as well as those that will come in the future.

Who wouldn't be willing to die for that!

14

A New Breed of Martyrs

1

Let's face it.

I shall never finish this book as long as I can be reached by phone, cable, telex or automobile. My gardener's cottage, with its picture window looking down on the old mill and the waterfall here in Canada, has become a 'command post' for constant uninterrupted dispatches from the front. I have already revised the manuscript several times. There is no end to it. The persecutions continue both in intensity and savagery.

My wife, Marguerite, who made the many journeys in Iran with me, is waiting for me to join her in Africa. Unless I pull out the phone and refuse to answer the doorbell, it doesn't look as though I'll have the chance.

This book was properly titled *A Cry from the Heart.*

Little did I know when I began to write it that, from the beginning to the end, my own heart would be stabbed with the pain of cablegram after cablegram, phone call after phone call, letter after letter, messenger after messenger, each one conveying the sad news of a fresh tragedy.

I have decided to go back to Africa, and to finish the book there, come what may.

* * *

I am now in Africa, and it is from this 'Continent of Light' that I have brought my book to an end with these final pages.

Unfortunately, Africa is Canada. Nothing has changed. The red river of sacrifice continues to stain the sands of Iran.

Even at this late date, the persecutors in Iran feel confident that they can hide their genocidal plot from the world. They hope to avoid a replay of the grave trouble and shame with which they were branded by the United Nations and the various governments of the world and the leaders of men back in 1955.

World opinion *does* cut down their options.

2

The masquerade is over!

It has been a rewarding experience to write this book, and to have the chance, however limited, to fight back.

Not with guns, knives, stones and clubs, which are the favourite weapons of the enemies of the Bahá'í Faith in Iran, but with words. Bahá'ís, as you know by now, are peace-loving, law-abiding and non-violent.

So, instead, I used a few violent words.

Words such as 'shame' and 'dishonour', and perhaps the most violent word of all:

'*Truth!*'

That always puts the liars on the run.

I took the advice of their own wonderful Prophet, the Apostle of God, Muhammad, when I did this.

Muhammad, whom they say the Bahá'í community in Iran is against, is *really* on the side of these innocent Bahá'í victims.

Any impartial observer would know that.

The Apostle of God, Muhammad, commands: '*Let there be no compulsion in religion.*' (Koran 2:257)

'Deny your faith,' the masked executioners demand.

'Never.'

'Just say you are *not* Bahá'ís, and I will save your lives.'

'Never!'

The executioners fire to kill. Remember Yazd and the other cities.

The Apostle of God, Muhammad, warned them:

> *What! wilt thou compel men to become believers? No soul can believe but by the permission of God: and he shall lay his wrath on those who will not understand.*
> (Koran 10:99–100)

Throughout this book, I have followed the advice of their Prophet Muhammad, whom *they,* not the Bahá'ís, have so shamefully disgraced by their conduct. The Apostle of God declared:

> *Nay, we will hurl the truth at falsehood, and it shall smite it, and lo! it shall vanish.*
> (Koran 21:18)

Our *Cry from the Heart* has done just that.

We have refuted every false charge, every baseless accusation, and every fraudulent misrepresentation made against the Bahá'ís in Iran.

They are not only refuted, but, as promised, demolished. It was my intention from the beginning to shoot down in flames the false accusers – non-violently, of course – with the truth about their obvious falsehoods.

For them, as far as world opinion goes, the masquerade is over!

There remains only my own deep feeling that I have not yet fulfilled the entire purpose of this book. It will not be complete until I have shared with you my thoughts on the spectre now haunting our society – the concern every man feels about the immediate survival of the entire human race – and the part played in this planetary tragedy by the Bahá'í martyrs of Iran.

Whose shadow is it that suddenly and unexpectedly appears on the radar screens of our countries?

Is it a friend? Or an enemy?

Each time we listen to the radio, watch television, or read the newspapers about the latest summit conference where the leaders of all nations have gathered for their crisis deliberation, we know those consultations could prove 'terminal' to our civilization.

We wonder as we gaze at the doors behind which they are trying to prevent a world catastrophe:

Who will come out? The lady or the tiger?

The remarkable and generally unknown role played by those seemingly insignificant and unimportant martyrs, dying almost every day in nearly every part of Iran, is both germane and vital to our own survival. What is happening to them concerns everything that is happening in the world.

I would be gravely remiss if I failed to share with you this astonishing, even incredible story. It has a message of hope and encouragement for every sad and disillusioned soul who is bewildered by the dreadful things taking place all around us today.

Although these martyrs are staining the sands of Iran red with their blood, they are, at the same time, nourishing the soil of a special *Tree of Life,* whose branches are already beginning to bring healing to the whole of humankind. This story gives meaning to their death and sacrifice, and in place of sorrow, you will find your heart gladdened with *good news* for a change.

The following personal and intimate thoughts are perhaps by far the most important and significant pages of this entire book.

3

The real pollution

What is it that makes the martyrdom of these Bahá'í

friends of mine in Iran so different? Why should the world care whether they live or die? Apart, that is, from the natural sorrow and sympathy all decent human beings feel who deplore killing, persecution, and violence of any kind.

After all, people are being killed all over the world these days. Violence and murder surround us every day of our lives. In the newspapers, on radio and television, we see and hear the dreadful things happening to our fellow human beings.

Since six million innocent Jews died so tragically and so wrongly in the murder-chambers of Nazi Germany, martyrdom has become almost an empty phrase.

People, unfortunately, have become inured to killing. They shut themselves off. They are weary of reading, hearing, and being told stories about more killings, more violence and death.

So why should the world be concerned about, or involved in, the martyrdoms of a few thousand Bahá'ís in Iran over the past years?

It is difficult for people to believe when first they hear it, that the murders committed by the terrorists of Iran are not only crimes against the Bahá'í community, but also crimes against society. It is not a local tragedy that is taking place behind that black-bordered death-map of Iran, but a world calamity.

Every passing day, MAN is becoming one of the most seriously 'endangered species' in the world. His chances of survival are becoming less and less. He is being threatened increasingly from every side.

The nuclear bombs, the multi-warhead intercontinental missiles with their nose-cones of death, plus all the other terrible weapons of war which he, man himself, has devised, might easily vaporize and obliterate both the fashioner and all his cities one of these days, taking most of the world, including us, with him.

In the face of such an inexcusable, horrifying, self-inflicted genocide, the extermination of a small religious minority in Iran would seem to be of no great significance.

It might *not* be so important were it not that this religious minority in Iran may be the only available source of spiritual 'fire power' in the world today, which is capable of rescuing mankind from the apparently certain destruction now facing it.

This religious minority has already proved, incredible as it may seem, that it indeed *does* have this spiritual power. At best, it could mitigate the approaching catastrophe if used properly. At the very worst, it can help some small remnant of society to survive the world-wide devastation which now threatens to engulf us all – inevitably unless something marvellous and miraculous happens soon.

To expect such a fantastic accomplishment from a minority religious community, being killed right and left at the will of their enemies, sounds a little like setting a *mouse* to drive the formidable elephant from the field!

Yet, this is exactly what this Bahá'í community has been doing for the past century and a half. In spite of the combined forces of the government, the army, the religious leaders, and the people of Iran, who have tried unsuccessfully to exterminate and obliterate them from the face of the earth, the Bahá'ís have not only survived, but have spread their message of love and unity to over one hundred thousand places in the world. It all began right there in Iran, and the struggle for survival – not of the Bahá'í community, but of the human race – continues as the gallant soldiers fall in battle.

Anyone truly conversant with the sacred Scriptures of the world would not be surprised at all. It is not the plan of man, but the Plan of God. This is exactly what has been promised to the world for this day in all the Holy Books.

I know that such a religious concept immediately puts

many people off. They lose all interest. However, when it is the 'last train out of Madrid' for all humanity, perhaps a little patience will bear wondrous fruit. We've tried *man's* answers and solutions. Where has *that* got us? Right where we stand now. On the brink of an awesome abyss.

Why not try God's answer? Or, at least satisfy ourselves whether or not it *is* God's answer?

The 'spiritual fire power' we are talking about is a down-to-earth, every day, run-of-the-mill miracle.

The *real* pollution the world faces is not in the smog over our cities, not in the mercury, oil-spills, and other poisons to be found in our oceans, lakes and streams, not even in the cancer-causing additives in the food we eat, the liquids we drink, the insufficiently tested drugs we take with their terrifying side-effects. All these are nothing compared to the real pollution.

That pollution is in the hearts of men.

The hatreds, the prejudices, the greed, the corruption and graft, the unbridled pursuit of possessions, the desire for material things at any cost, these are the animal-like qualities which have always destroyed individuals, families, states, nations and civilizations. A decadent, overpowering, overwhelming, cancerous materialism now has all mankind in its iron grasp, and will not let go.

It will take a spiritual remedy to cure all that. Nothing else has, or we wouldn't be in all this trouble.

Fanaticism has no place in the Bahá'í Faith. Bahá'ís are expected to live a full, rich, wonderful life, experiencing its joy and wonder and awe, but always remembering their primary responsibilities to God and their fellow men.

When mankind forgets these responsibilities, he uses selfishly and to his own danger the great material, physical, and scientific gains the human mind has created. The proper use of these blessings depends on the heart and conscience of man. He can use these wonders to heal or to destroy.

That is the crisis.

Until this *real* pollution of hate, prejudice and greed in the heart of man is removed, our civilization will only continue its downward plunge toward that awesome abyss of death ahead.

Where can man turn for help?

Many thinking people are now beginning to wonder if perhaps we haven't paid too dearly for these material gains of ours, gains which, in one moment of caprice on the part of the world's leaders, could be swept away, leaving the world in ashes.

Visionless and unshepherded on a world scale, man in his plight proclaims his spiritual bankruptcy. So where can he turn for help in this planetary crisis?

Where is his ultimate hope?

4

Anything less than planetary is doomed to failure

In order to appreciate fully, and not to be too shocked at the concept of a small religious minority having the 'spiritual fire power' to come to the aid of a civilization and society in despair, it is necessary for us to examine the world at large and see if we can find any *other* source, anywhere, which can meet the crying needs of this afflicted world.

Let us examine every major possible hope the world can offer before contemplating such an apparently unlikely possibility.

Where else is our hope?

Can Science save us? Government? Politics? The United Nations? Education? Economics? Religion?

Which?

These are all we have.

Where among them can we hope to find a vision and a power vital and strong enough to rescue the world from an obvious onrushing, all-encompassing disaster?

There must be *some* way out.

Let us try each hope we can find, for the time is critical, and the need is desperate. We must find that way out, or perish.

Therefore, which of these 'last-ditch' hopes of the world shall we choose?

Science?

Science is neither good nor bad. It is neutral. It diminishes the death-rate of individuals on one hand by perfecting a wonder drug, a new serum, or open-heart surgery, and then, on the other hand, this same Science can destroy multitudes by fashioning nuclear weapons.

Science can be used for either constructive or destructive purposes. It depends upon the moral conscience of the men who use it. Again we come back to that inescapable *real* pollution in the hearts of men.

Science is an *instrument,* not an operator. Science is a ship, not the Captain. So it can never be the Master-Pilot of our hopes. It will never be able to guide us safely into the harbour of survival until we learn to use it properly.

What next?

Politics?

Which party? Of which country? Of a house or a planet divided?

Politics has been called the 'degenerate son' of an 'illustrious father', Statesmanship. In spite of many noble public servants and excellent politicians, who *do* endeavour to uphold the honour and value of politics, this corrupted son of a splendid father has become a wastrel, who is now too often given over to corruption, graft, policy, expediency, and the preservation of his own position and prestige at the expense of the well-being of both his party and his fellow men.

Politics too many times has abandoned virtue, and has forsaken its primary and vital role in building a safe refuge for all the peoples of the world while preserving the rights, prestige and dignity of each country.

Politics these days is generally a mortally sick and dying patient and not an administering doctor at all. Politics has clearly demonstrated that it is *not* our Master Physician and the Healer of our ills.

Government?

Which?

Democratic? Republican? Capitalistic? Communistic? Dictatorship? And all the other varieties?

Which?

Almost every government has much that is of value, much that is heroic, and a good measure that is quite wonderful.

Some governments certainly seem preferable to others. But it all depends on who is doing the preferring. Different governments for different people. All sincere. The choice of the best government often depends upon the circumstances and geography of a man or woman's birth and upbringing.

Unfortunately for mankind, there is no one single government in the entire world at the present time which has so captured the imagination, the devotion, and the allegiance of all the other nations of the world, that peoples everywhere are ready and willing to set aside their lesser loyalties in order to follow such an inspired leadership.

Some governments gave promise of being such world leaders in their early days. The lustre was lost with the passing of time. Governments became partisan instead of impartial, competitive instead of co-operative. In place of highways and open gates, they built hating-walls. The crises of our divided world deepened.

The world moved away from, rather than toward, unity.

Any plan that is less than planetary in this age is doomed to failure. Sectarian, limited viewpoints are meaningless in an age where world unity is essential for survival.

The governments of the world have still neither learned nor accepted this vital global lesson.

Government alone cannot rescue us.

Where else can man turn?

His options are diminishing rapidly.

Economics?

Is there an Economic Plan that can rescue and save the world?

This area is hardly worth exploring, for the bitter truth is that a wholesome system of economics is the *result* of a civilization, not the cause of it.

In order to have a wholesome economy, we must first create the social relationships which make co-operation on a planetary scale possible. We must have this international co-operative effort, everywhere, if we are to succeed.

If a family will not live together in love, harmony and co-operation, the income required to support it becomes double, treble, often quadruple what the united family would require.

This is equally true of the family of nations.

No member of a loving family would live in comfort and luxury in one room of the house while the other members were hungry, ill, abandoned and forgotten in another room.

This should also be true of the house of Nations, the planet on which we live.

Yet, we *do* live in that cruel and heartless manner, don't we?

As nations.

If we hope to solve the economic problems of the world, we must first set about healing the social relationships which now prevent us from becoming such a concerned family of nations.

We must somehow achieve a world-wide, close and loving co-operative spirit, one that will inspire us to pour out our resources for those things which will bring about a life-sustaining, hope-creating standard of living for all mankind. A world of hope for *all* our brothers and sisters, everywhere on earth. For we *are* that to each other, and we must treat each other as if we were all part of one great family.

We *have* the resources, we have the food, we have in abundance the material possessions needed for all humanity.

We even have the transportation.

We have almost *everything*.

What we *don't* have is the *Spirit*.

Obviously, we cannot find it in any economic plan or system, since economic justice is the *result* of a world in harmony, and not the creator of it. What is left to bring us safely through this galactic storm?

Only Education and Religion remain.

Which?

Education? Can Education save us?

Certainly it can help. However, the crisis in which the world now finds itself is a *moral,* not an *intellectual* crisis.

Education can guarantee knowledge, but it cannot guarantee wisdom. The most intellectually brilliant scholar can be cruel, selfish and unjust. Intellectual or technical education, no matter how broad or prolonged, cannot be depended upon to make men kind, generous or loving. Some of our so-called most advanced nations have proved to be the most ruthless, barbarous and deadly.

Education is certainly an essential and vital ingredient in establishing and maintaining this better world we seek, but it is obviously not the Master-Architect we desperately need in our hour of realized doom.

Education cannot save us.

Religion?

Which?

Christian? Jewish? Muslim? Hindu? Buddhist? Zoroastrian? Or any among all the others?

If Muslim, which sect? Shiah or Sunni?

If Jewish, which? Orthodox, Reformed or Conservative?

If Christian, which branch or sect? Catholic or Protestant or Greek Orthodox? If Protestant, which one of the several hundred existing sects? Anglican? Lutheran? Presbyterian? Baptist? Methodist? On and on they go.

There is no need to continue, the point is clear.

In *each* religion there is beauty, truth and power. Each is a *Way* and a *Path*. Each has accomplished miracles in the hearts of its followers.

But collectively they are disunited. There is even disunity within each one. After all, sects of the great religions are born because of *differences,* not agreement.

God made them one and progressive, as we have seen from our drawings in the chapter, 'The Banner of Islam'. Man has made them many.

A mirror shattered into pieces cannot be expected to reflect the full, bright, shining light of the sun. Only a flash, a glimmering is seen, although still beautiful enough to capture hearts.

No sincere person would ever belittle the personal comfort which each of these great religions brings to the individuals who believe in them. Yet, neither would any sincere person deny their apparent helplessness in dealing effectively with the grave social problems which are tormenting this perilous age. Religion is unable to deal with the planetary problems facing today's world. It has been unable to heal the wounds in its own divided and separated body.

How then can we expect it to bind up the broken limbs of a sceptical and disbelieving society?

Where then do we turn?

What is left?

The United Nations!

It chills the heart to think that even this marvellous accomplishment of the human race, the United Nations, may not be able to save us after all.

The United Nations was once the 'darling of our hearts'!

No fair-minded man would ever deny its wonderful victories in so many fields. Who can fail to appreciate the fires it has put out, the threats it has averted, or the ominous catastrophes it has delayed? Its great services in the areas of World Health, World Bank, Unesco, Unicef, Catastrophe Relief, Economic Assistance, and many other splendid areas of service, are brilliant and unquestioned.

Yet, in the most vital area of all, the important political area, which determines the survival of every human being on the planet, our old friends Partisan, National, Hemisphere, Group and Block-of-Nations Politics eat remorselessly away at the framework day by day.

There is no need to catalogue the various conflicts, divisions, and tactics which now threaten the ultimate survival of this slowly-fading hope of the world.

The lustre of those 'golden days' in San Francisco is long forgotten. The world-wide joy of those happy hours, when the Charter was written and the blue-and-white Flag of World Peace was fashioned, has dimmed.

There is no longer that exciting *spell* of World-Oneness that brightened our hopes and cheered our hearts. Gone is the sense of unity and determination, in spite of basic differences, that assured the peoples of the world that our planet was at last in safe hands for the future, and we could put aside the haunting spectre of a Third World War.

What days they were!

Gradually, our United Nations has become like the Cat in Aesop's Fable. The Cat was permitted to attend the great Banquet Hall dressed as a beautiful damsel, provided it would remember to behave properly.

So, in like manner, do the leaders of the world's nations attend the critical conference tables, dressed up as lovers of mankind, expressing concern for the welfare of all nations and peoples, as well as for their own.

Until, suddenly, the '*Mouse of Spoils!*' – Power, Prestige, Position, Advantage – runs across the banquet table in front of them.

Zoom! A Cat again!

It is beginning to appear that the printer, who made the unfortunate typographical error with his linotype machine at San Francisco, was prophetic.

On the day of the signing of the United Nations Charter, he misplaced the letter "I" in one of the newspaper headlines. Instead of writing: THE UNITED NATIONS, he typed: THE UNTIED NATIONS.

That great world-protecting *knot* has been slipping, little by little, more and more, since those early days of great expectancy. It has been slowly loosened by the increasing hostility of the contending nations.

The looser the knot becomes, the greater grows the danger.

The world still rests its hopes in and supports the United Nations, and sacrifices generously for its survival. It remains the very best of all we have. But the United Nations cannot save us.

Not until the 'pollution' in the hearts of its members has been replaced by the wholesome, selfless virtues needed to put the *world,* not their own nations, first in all their deliberations, will it be successful.

It is, after all, a United *Nations,* not Nation.

That wonderful body can delay, it can soften, it can win us precious time, but it cannot prevent the inevitable, all-consuming disaster that slowly and resistlessly approaches in spite of all we do.

What might *once* have been, now will never be.

What a tragedy it is, that we must look elsewhere.

We were so close!

5

A vision of things to come

What has all this background on the United Nations to do with the current martyrdom of so many Bahá'ís in Yazd, Shiraz, Tabriz, Teheran and Hamadan?

Everything!

In fact, it will bring into focus all that I have written thus far. It will help us to understand *why* I have repeated so many times that they are a *new breed* of martyrs, unique and special, and why their deaths are of significance to everyone, and not just to their fellow Bahá'ís.

Over one hundred years ago, Bahá'u'lláh, Founder of the Bahá'í Faith, wrote to the rulers and leaders of men, the Heads of State of that day, calling upon them to raise up a World Body, which would foster the growth of a world community. Bahá'u'lláh described the character and purpose of this Body. He said that it would have the primary responsibility of establishing an enduring peace among men.

Bahá'u'lláh did far more than merely *call* for its establishment. He offered to the world's leaders the laws, principles, institutions, agencies and guidance which would enable them to raise up, preserve and maintain this world peace. Above all, He brought the *Spirit* to make it all work.*

Unwittingly, unaware of the Source that drove them on

* That, of course, is but *one* facet of the great world spiritual 'force' released by Bahá'u'lláh. This Commonwealth of all nations would rule in justice the entire earth, and exercise 'unchallengeable authority over its unimaginably vast resources, blending and embodying the ideals of both the East and the West, liberated from the curse of war and its miseries, and bent on the exploitation of all the available sources of energy on the surface of the planet, a system in which Force is made the servant of Justice' – a world dedicated to the safety, security and happiness of all peoples on the planet, without preference, without exception.

to their destiny, completely ignoring the guidance they had received, the nations of the world *twice* made an effort to establish this 'Union of Nations' as it was called in the Bahá'í writings. First, the *League of Nations*; then, in a far more concentrated world-wide effort, the United Nations as we know it today.

Unfortunately for mankind, the nations of the world, in their attempts to establish a World Consultative Body, followed only a *part* of Bahá'u'lláh's guidance. As a result, they achieved only *part* of their possible success.

How tragic that they didn't follow it all.

It is one of the most fascinating, but ironic twists of history that mankind should have been on the very threshold of one of the most significant and major discoveries of all time. The information which the nations of the world needed, to assure their safety and survival on the planet, had already been placed in the hands of the leaders of their countries. It was a veritable '*mother-lode*' of Truth and Guidance, a spiritual 'force' which was completely capable of meeting head-on, and resolving the terrifying and paralyzing problems that weighed the world down.

They failed each time to recognize its true worth.

This 'Pearl of Great Price', as sacred Scripture called it, this treasured gift of nation-healing, was ignored, to the peril of us all.

Several of the Fourteen Points which President Woodrow Wilson presented, in launching his concept of the League of Nations, fairly breathed the spirit of Bahá'u'lláh's teachings on World Unity.

The President was familiar with the writings of Bahá'u'lláh. Many of the concepts were there, but the Source remained unrecognized and unmentioned. That Source which, alone, could deliver the spiritual 'fire power' absolutely essential to the success of the entire venture. The League struggled but failed in its prime task of securing peace. Although it laid the foundations of great world agencies, it could not prevent the militarism which finally led to World War II.

That was the *first* attempt.

The story of the *second* attempt, the founding of the United Nations, is far more intimately and dramatically interwoven with the fortunes and the fate of both humanity and the Bahá'í Faith. It is told in detail elsewhere.* Here, we touch only the briefest highlights.

California, site of the great United Nations Conference where the Charter was written and its blue-and-white flag was raised, had already been designated for this honour in the writings of the Bahá'í Faith – long before the event took place.

'Abdu'l-Bahá, the appointed successor of Bahá'u'lláh, uttered these prophetic words in the shadow of San Francisco: 'May the first flag of International Peace be upraised in this State ...'

It all came true, with the exactness of the stars.

One of the most interesting links between the Bahá'í Faith and the emergence of the United Nations is seen in Bahá'u'lláh's addresses to the rulers and leaders of mankind. Especially four remarkable and historic documents.

To whom were these *four* documents written?

To the rulers of the four countries who were designated as *four out of the five* 'Permanent Members' of the Security Council of the United Nations.

Imagine!

The rulers of Britain, France, Russia and the United States (China was the fifth) received these special messages from Bahá'u'lláh, concerning the responsibilities of the nations and their leaders towards the vital needs of the emerging world society of the present day.

In His letter to Queen Victoria, Bahá'u'lláh called upon

* See *'Abdu'l-Bahá* by Hasan Balyuzi (George Ronald, Oxford, 1971), pp. 312–13; and *The Prisoner and the Kings* by William Sears (General Publishing Co. Ltd. Toronto).

the rulers of the earth to be reconciled among themselves, to reduce their armaments, and to be united so that their peoples might 'find rest'. He advised them to take counsel together: 'Let your concern be only for that which profiteth mankind and bettereth the condition thereof...' His Mission, He told them, was 'to regenerate and unify mankind.'

In many of Bahá'u'lláh's writings this ringing call was made. He emphasized the absolute necessity, the utter urgency of establishing a World Body, and declared that the time had come for the calling together of 'a vast, an all-embracing assemblage of men' so that the rights of all nations and peoples might be assured, and the peace of the world, at long last, become a reality. He even gave clear guidance concerning the steps such a body of nations should follow to achieve the protection and permanent security of mankind.

All these dramatic events are inseparably linked to the story of the present-day martyrs in Iran.

Every additional bit of background information on the Bahá'í Faith and its relationship to the world and its peoples increases our understanding of why no true Bahá'í in Iran, or anywhere else in the world, would ever think of renouncing his Faith.

It is too wonderful to give up.

He or she would rather die first, and thus become part of that forward momentum and spiritual 'fire power' that is speeding God's Plan on its way to fulfilment on the entire surface of the planet.

Bahá'u'lláh offered the world in His writings clear and convincing solutions for the troubles and problems it would soon have to deal with, many of which were unforeseen except by Him.*

* The fascinating story of Bahá'u'lláh's letters to the leaders of men, and the solutions He offered to their problems, can be found in: *The Promised Day is Come,* by Shoghi Effendi (Bahá'í Publishing Trust, Wilmette, Illinois, rev. 1961), and *The Proclamation of Bahá'u'lláh,* by Bahá'u'lláh (Bahá'í World Centre, Haifa, 1967), both of which describe this thrilling and dramatic story of His 'call to the nations'.

Such problems as:

1. The threat of global war.
2. The mad race to fashion ever-greater weapons of destruction which could 'poison' the atmosphere and destroy the cities.
3. The need to reduce armaments to the measure necessary to safeguard internal security, and, in partnership with all other nations, to police the world.
4. Seething racial tension.
5. Corruption and graft in government, politics, and business.
6. The weakening and dissolution of marriage ties, and the grievous disintegration of family life.
7. Widespread crime and violence, intensifying everywhere.
8. The alarming increase in mental illness of all kinds.
9. The even more alarming world-wide increase in the use of alcohol.
10. The terrifying, soul-destroying, mind-damaging wounds caused by an unparalleled increase in the use of habit-forming drugs.
11. Religion's failure to solve personal and social problems.
12. The growing threat of atheism.
13. The mounting conflict between capital and labour.
14. The increasing discrepancy between rich and poor.

This vision of 'things to come' by Bahá'u'lláh is not at all surprising, when we remember that He has called upon all His followers in the Bahá'í world to arise and help establish that *'Christ-promised Kingdom of God on earth'*.

Christ had clearly foretold that the *'Spirit of Truth'*, when He should come, would lead men 'unto all truth', and inform them of those many things which they were unable to hear long centuries ago.

Bahá'u'lláh has done all that, and more.

Small wonder then that the humblest believers in Iran, who truly love both the Báb and Bahá'u'lláh, and all Their teachings, would scornfully reply: *'No!'* to the executioners who try to get them to deny their Faith. They answer today exactly as the uncle of the Báb answered the Prime Minister of Iran, who had sentenced him to death in Teheran unless he would recant his Faith.

He said firmly:

'If I refuse to acknowledge the mission of the Báb, I must also deny the divine character of the message which Muhammad, Jesus, Moses and all the Prophets of the past have revealed. God knows that whatever I have heard and read concerning the lives of these past Messengers of God, the same have I been privileged to witness from this Youth, this beloved Kinsman of mine, from His earliest boyhood to this, the thirtieth year of His life. I only request that you allow me to be the first to lay down my life in His path.'

The Prime Minister, stupefied by such an answer, without uttering a word, motioned that the Báb's uncle should be taken out and beheaded.*

Already, over one hundred and thirty years ago, they were a *new breed* of martyrs who died on behalf of all religions, all the Messengers of God, and all the nations and peoples they represented.

I hope that some day you will read each one of their remarkable and thrilling stories, concerning the fulfilment of the promise of all ages and the founding of the Kingdom of God on earth.

---

* The full story of this uncle of the Báb, Ḥájí Mírzá Siyyid 'Alí, may be read in Nabíl's Narrative, *The Dawn-Breakers* (US edn.), pp. 446–9. His words as given here are a close paraphrase.

6

'Release the chains!'

We are approaching the end of our journey.

I think you will agree that the story behind the martyrdoms in Iran, explaining why the Bahá'í heroes and heroines die so willingly, would have been both incomplete and inaccurate, their cruel and senseless murders quite incomprehensible, if we had not shared with you this background.

They are *not* just part of the Islamic Revolution, nor part of the plan of the present regime in Iran; they are part of the Plan of God.

There is quite a difference.

There remain only two things for me to do before ending this *Cry from the Heart*. Both are quite pleasing, and are equally intriguing.

One: Make clear exactly *why* there have been nearly one hundred and fifty years of persecution and death for the Bahá'í community in Iran.

Two: Demonstrate that there *is* already functioning in the world a *microcosm* – the Bahá'í World Community – which has successfully met and overcome the society-destroying sicknesses, evils and conflicts which beset and divide the world at large.

There *is* a place to turn to for an answer. One which has already proved that it can do the job, however big, involved, or seemingly insoluble.

You may not be the least bit religious, but can you afford to ignore a community which, in more than one hundred thousand places in the world, has turned hate into love, fear into courage, despondency into hope, and indifference into enthusiastic service on behalf of the entire human race?

So, let's start racing toward the end.

First: why have the persecutions and deaths of the Bahá'ís in Iran gone on so long?

The answer is quite simple.

The goal, which the Bahá'ís everywhere on the planet have set themselves to achieve, is of incomparable greatness.

It is to bring about the organic unity of all nations, races, religions and peoples. One great peaceful, prosperous, progressive human society, with differences harmonized and aspirations blended into one common effort.

Therefore, the preparation and sacrifice for such a tremendous accomplishment must be equally as great as the goal itself. A mighty structure takes infinitely more time and trouble to raise up than a smaller one. The Bahá'ís are building the *Kingdom of God on earth,* and this is the long-awaited and promised *Day of the One Fold and One Shepherd.*

What we are talking about is a tremendous Event in the history of the world. Unique. Peerless. Unprecedented. A Day of incomparable greatness.

The sacrifice required to usher in such an unprecedented age of World Unity is likewise of the same heroic proportions.

It has involved the Herald of this new Day, as well as the Founder.

The Báb sacrificed His life for all the Prophets gone before. Bahá'u'lláh, in His turn, the Promised One of all religions, races, nations and peoples, offered up *His* life throughout half a century of persecution. It is a story the like of which the ears of men have never heard. So great was Their love for the Messengers who prepared the way for Them that it cannot be contained in the words of man.

Bahá'u'lláh felt this tender, inexpressible love for *all* God's Messengers. He wrote about Them so often and so lovingly, and He took upon Himself all Their sufferings. He was exiled like Abraham, He was stoned like Moses, He was scourged like Christ. For forty long years, exactly as foretold in Scripture, He endured the agony of a fresh affliction almost every day.*

He was once scourged, twice stoned, three times imprisoned, four times exiled. He was poisoned on three separate occasions. He was weighted down with hundred-pound chains that tore His flesh and scarred His body all the remaining days of His life. His feet were placed in stocks. He was chained to the floor and to His companions in an underground dungeon-prison. He was in mortal danger all His life.

Yet every attempt made upon Bahá'u'lláh's life by the authorities in Iran, and His enemies in other places, was frustrated. God had other plans. In spite of all their schemes and machinations, Bahá'u'lláh came at last to the Holy Land, and to Carmel, the Mountain and Vineyard of God. It was the place destined for Him by God from the beginning of history.

The Father, the *Lord of the Vineyard*, had come home at last!

From His cell in the fortress-prison of 'Akka, Bahá'u'lláh wrote on behalf of *all* the Messengers of God:

> The Ancient Beauty hath consented to be bound with chains that mankind may be released from its bondage, and hath accepted to be made a prisoner within this most mighty Stronghold that the whole world may attain unto true liberty. He hath drained to its dregs the cup of sorrow, that all the peoples of the earth may attain unto abiding joy, and be filled with gladness. This is of the mercy of your Lord, the Compassionate, the Most Merciful. We have accepted to be abased, O believers in the Unity of God, that ye may be exalted, and have suffered manifold afflictions, that ye might prosper and flourish.

That is the answer to the question, *Why* have the Bahá'í

* See Psalms 95:10

persecutions and martyrdoms gone on for such a long time in Iran? It was the Cradle of this World Religion, the scene of the first battles, where the trenches were dug deep into the soil of the human heart. No day has ever been like it or ever will be again.

The sacrifice is commensurate.

7

Microcosm, Macrocosm!

You might call the Bahá'ís in their hundred-thousand communities around the world the 'spiritual mutants' of this age, for they have already demonstrated their ability to change hate into love, prejudice into admiration, indifference into enthusiasm, and neglect into involvement. Through the Spirit with which Bahá'u'lláh, the Founder of their Faith, has imbued them, they have been able to change the hearts of men, something far more difficult to do than changing copper into gold.

The need to change the hearts of mankind is devastatingly apparent everywhere; the Bahá'ís are working that very miracle every day of their lives all over the planet. The world could find no more hopeful or encouraging example anywhere than that offered every day in the Bahá'í communities around the world.

Already, in their growing microcosm of a world community, the Bahá'ís have won victories which humanity is still desperately and unsuccessfully struggling to achieve. Already they have resolved devastating racial differences, desolating religious prejudices, and have conquered those seemingly unconquerable hatreds, all of which now threaten the entire macrocosm of the world.

Where else can mankind find another such proof that it *can* be done?

But just how effective is it?

A world in despair might think about this:

Bahá'ís already have Arabs and Jews working together

side by side in their local communities, not necessarily in Chicago or London or Buenos Aires where it might be safe, but in those very areas of the world where members of these races stand ready, poised, and prepared to kill and annihilate each other.

Bahá'ís of Christian and Muslim backgrounds now live together in peace and active participation in the Bahá'í communities of Lebanon.

Irish and British Bahá'ís in Northern Ireland, once Catholic and Protestant, are one in spirit and love for each other. They serve together harmoniously, with genuine affection and co-operation, in their Bahá'í local communities in that land.

The same holds true of the black and the white in Africa, and in the southern States of the United States.

The *Spirit* of the Bahá'í Faith has captured their hearts, and transformed their former hatreds and antagonisms into love and unity, genuine and sincere. They work together happily, with laughter and a new-found joy, in enthusiastic co-operation.

This also holds true of capitalist and communist, East and West, rich and poor, old and young, passive and dominant – they have all forsaken their former limited and defensive isolated positions in order to allow the *Spirit* of Bahá'u'lláh to take over and transform their lives.

They are indeed a 'new race' of men and women.

They are only too happy to give up everything in life to be a part of this wonderful, healing, hope-restoring Kingdom of God on earth. Not tomorrow, or in some far-off day. But *now,* today, when the world needs it.

This is not some vague day of religious mystery and wonder that we are talking about, a Kingdom that would descend in some strange way from the clouds.

Not on your life!

This is a world in which every person on earth will be motivated, for a change, by his *human,* his *moral,* his *ethical,* and his *spiritual* virtues. Not by his animal nature, as we see happening so grossly in the darkened world around us. A world in which every man, woman and child will be able to develop the latent talents and gifts with which God has so generously endowed them. Where education will be for all on the planet who wish it, *really* for all. Where *have* and *have-not* people, and *have* and *have-not* nations will no longer exist.

We have become a pleasure-seeking society, not a truth-seeking society. We should be both. We have become a profit-making, rather than a welfare-producing society. We should be both.

We should be balanced. Natural human beings living full, rich, useful lives of happiness and service, surrounded by the warming love and comfort of our families and neighbours.

It is *this* world the Bahá'í community wants everyone to enjoy. This is the world for which every Bahá'í martyr in Iran, and all Bahá'ís everywhere on the planet, are sacrificing their time, their resources, their energies, and, if necessary, their lives.

It is the long-awaited, and universally foretold *Kingdom of God on earth.*

That's *worth* dying for, isn't it?

Incidentally, I've changed my mind.

I *do* want something from you.

I'm holding in my hand yet *another cablegram*!

I was on my way to mail these final chapters when I found it waiting for me in my Post Office box.

It tells of the martyrdom of six more dear Bahá'í friends under unspeakable conditions, five on the very day I finished this book. One in Teheran, five more in Darun, a village near Isfahan.

Same false charges, same illegal executions by firing-squads. Only *this* time, they tried to hide the entire murderous project. No announcement of the killings was made.

The pressure of the world is beginning to tell, but their 'well-organized, carefully conceived, ruthlessly implemented plan of extermination' goes remorselessly on.

As I write the final revised paragraphs of this book, I say farewell to:

> Ḥabíbu'lláh 'Azízí in Teheran,
> Bahman 'Áṭifí,
> 'Izzat 'Áṭifí,
> 'Aṭá'u'lláh Rawḥání,
> Aḥmad Riḍvání,
> and Thábit Rásikh, all in Darun.

The families of these dear innocent victims were not even informed of the executions. Their relatives were not permitted to conduct Bahá'í funerals for their loved ones. Three of these dear souls were buried unceremoniously in Muslim graves.

However secretly and insidiously the fanatics in Iran behave, it is only a secret to them. Already the Bahá'í World Community in all the continents of the globe is sharing the 'secret' with the press, radio, television, newspapers and governments.

It is this cablegram, and the last one from Hamadan describing the tortures inflicted on the bodies of my friends there, that still haunt me.

These are what make me change my mind. I *do* want something – a brief prayer.

Whenever you think of it, or whenever it's convenient. Just: 'O God! Protect the innocent Bahá'ís.'

The way I look at it, since this book will be read by people everywhere in the world, that should add up to a lot of prayers. Particularly if they are Hindu, Buddhist, Zoroastrian, Jewish, Muslim, Christian, Catholic, Baptist, Lutheran, Methodist, Presbyterian, Anglican and American Indian.

Keep the good thought!

My book is over.

It was never authoritative, nor was it official. It was always personal. My own heartfelt cry of indignation at what was happening to some of the finest, sweetest and dearest people ever placed on the planet.

This book was for them, my friends.

It was also for you, one of that overwhelming number of sincere souls who still belong to the human race.

My reward is that you and your friends have finally heard my *Cry from the Heart*.

> A cry from the heart: 'How long, O Lord?
> How long? How long is justice hidden?'
> 'Till the very end,' the Lord replied.
> 'Till *all* is won, as God has bidden.'

May that day come soon.

15

Names

Many other dear friends have been arrested, imprisoned, executed and interrogated. Some were released. At least temporarily. Some were kidnapped, their whereabouts still unknown. Others still remain in prison awaiting their fate.

I have not circled their names. Not yet.

May I never have to do so.

You need not dwell on the names. This part of the book is for me. I merely wanted you to see their names as you skim rapidly through these pages.

Very few people believe in anything these days. Belief in God has dwindled considerably. I mean such a belief in God that you are willing to die for it. Therefore, the names on this *Honour Roll* carry a special fragrance and a blessing for the eyes.

These names are difficult to pronounce for a westerner who is not familiar with Farsi (Persian), but how sweet to the ear is the sound of the names of heroes!

No wonder the Bahá'ís the world over love the Persian people. Especially *these* Persian people who rank among the finest of all Iranians.

Fathers, mothers, husbands, wives, children, all gave up their lives rather than give up their belief in Bahá'u'lláh and the Bahá'í Faith. Willingly, valiantly, enthusiastically.

No wonder I have put them on my Honour Roll so their names will be seen by their fellow Bahá'ís in every part of the world. I wanted to give them the honour of your seeing their names as well, if only a brief glimpse in passing.

What a pity to impoverish the land and lose all this love and dedication.

BAHÁ'ÍS KILLED IN IRAN SINCE 1978

As of 15 December, 1981

(Published as received from official sources)

A number of those listed were members of Bahá'í institutions, indicated as follows: Continental Board of Counsellors (CBC); Auxiliary Board (AB); National Spiritual Assembly (NSA); Local Spiritual Assembly (LSA).

No.	Date	Name	Place	Remarks
1.	1978	Mr Aḥmad Ismá'íli	Ahram	Killed
2.	12 Aug. 1978	Mr Díyá'u'lláh Ḥaqíqat	Jahrum	Intentionally run over and killed by motor-cycle
3.	27 Aug. 1978	Mr Naw-Rúzí	Shahmírzád	Burned to death
4.	27 Aug. 1978	Mr Akhaván-i-Kathírí	Shahmírzád	Burned to death
5.	10 Oct. 1978	Mr Ḥájí-Muḥammad 'Azízí	Khurmúj	Beaten to death
6.	Dec. 1978	Mr Ḥátam Rúzbihí	Búyir-Aḥmad	Killed by mobs
7.	Dec. 1978	Mr Ján-'Alí Rúzbihí	Búyir-Aḥmad	Killed by mobs
8.	Dec. 1978	Mr Shír-Muḥammad Dastpísh	Búyir-Aḥmad	Killed by mobs
9.	14 Dec. 1978	Mr Ṣifátu'lláh Fahandízh	Shíráz	Mobbed in incident in Sa'díyyih
10.	14 Dec. 1978	Mrs Fahandízh		
11.	22 Dec. 1978	Mr Parvíz Afnání	Miyán-Du'áb	Killed by mobs and bodies burned
12.	22 Dec. 1978	Mr Khusraw Afnání		

13.	Early 1979	Mr Ibráhím Ma'naví	Hiṣár, Khurásán	Killed
14.	2 Apr. 1979	Mr Ḥusayn Shakúrí	Ushnavíyyih	Killed
15.	27 Sep. 1979	Mr Bahár Vujdání	Mahábád	Executed
16.	28 Oct. 1979	Mr 'Alí Sattárzádih	Búkán	Killed
17.	14 Dec. 1979	Mr 'Azamatu'lláh Fahandizh	Shíráz	Executed
18.	4 Feb. 1980	Mr Ḥabíbu'lláh Panáhí	Urúmíyyih	Assassinated
19.	6 May 1980	Mr Ghulám-Ḥusayn A'ẓamí	Teheran	Executed
20.	6 May 1980	Mr Badí'u'lláh Yazdání	Teheran	Executed
21.	6 May 1980	Mr 'Alí-Akbar Mu'íní	Teheran	Executed
22.	9 May 1980	Mr 'Alí-Akbar Khursandí	Teheran	Tortured and hanged
23.	11 May 1980	Mr Parvíz Bayání	Píránshahr	Executed
24.	18 May 1980	Mr Mír-Asadu'lláh Mukhtárí	Andrún, Bírjand	Stoned to death
25.	June 1980	Mr Ḥasan Ismá'ílzádih	Sanandaj	Killed
26.	27 June 1980	Mr Yúsuf Subḥání	Teheran	Executed
27.	14 July 1980	Dr Farámarz Samandarí	Tabríz	Executed (LSA)
28.	14 July 1980	Mr Yadu'lláh Ástání	Tabríz	Executed (LSA)
29.	16 July 1980	Mr 'Alí Dádásh-Akbarí	Rasht	Executed (LSA)
30.	30 July 1980	Mr Yadu'lláh Maḥbúbíyán	Teheran	Executed
31.	15 Aug. 1980	Mr Dhabíhu'lláh Mu'miní	Teheran	Executed
32.	8 Sep. 1980	Mr Núru'lláh Akhtar-Khávarí	Yazd	Executed (LSA)
33.	8 Sep. 1980	Mr Maḥmúd Ḥasanzádih	Yazd	Executed (LSA)
34.	8 Sep. 1980	Mr 'Azízu'lláh Dhabíhíyán	Yazd	Executed (AB)
35.	8 Sep. 1980	Mr Firaydún Farídání	Yazd	Executed (AB)

No.	Date	Name	Place	Remarks
36.	8 Sep. 1980	Mr 'Abdu'l-Vahháb Kázimí Mansháḍí	Yazd	Executed (LSA)
37.	8 Sep. 1980	Mr Jalál Mustaqím	Yazd	Executed (LSA)
38.	8 Sep. 1980	Mr 'Alí Mutahharí	Yazd	Executed (LSA)
39.	9 Nov. 1980	Mr Riḍá Fírúzí	Tabríz	Executed
40.	22 Nov. 1980	Mr Muḥammad-Ḥusayn Ma'ṣúmí	Núk, Bírjand	Burned to death
41.	22 Nov. 1980	Mrs Shikkar-Nisá' Ma'ṣúmí	Núk, Bírjand	Burned to death
42.	17 Dec. 1980	Mr Bihrúz Saná'í	Teheran	Executed
43.	12 Jan. 1981	Dr Manúchihr Ḥakím	Teheran	Assassinated
44.	17 Mar. 1981	Mr Mihdí Anvarí	Shíráz	Executed
45.	17 Mar. 1981	Mr Hidáyatu'lláh Dihqání	Shíráz	Executed
46.	Apr. 1981	Mrs Núráníyyih Yársháṭir	Teheran	Assassinated
47.	30 Apr. 1981	Mr Yadu'lláh Vaḥdat	Shíráz	Executed (AB)
48.	30 Apr. 1981	Mr Sattár Khushkhú	Shíráz	Executed
49.	30 Apr. 1981	Mr Iḥsánu'lláh Mihdí-Zádih	Shíráz	Executed
50.	14 June 1981	Mr Suhráb (Muḥammad) Ḥabíbí	Hamadán	Executed (LSA)
51.	14 June 1981	Mr Ḥusayn Khándil	Hamadán	Executed (LSA)
52.	14 June 1981	Mr Ṭaráẓu'lláh Khuzayn	Hamadán	Executed (LSA)
53.	14 June 1981	Dr Fírúz Na'ímí	Hamadán	Executed (LSA)
54.	14 June 1981	Dr Náṣir Vafá'í	Hamadán	Executed (LSA)
55.	14 June 1981	Mr Suhayl (Muḥammad-Báqir) Ḥabíbí	Hamadán	Executed (LSA)

No.	Date	Name	Place	Fate
56.	14 June 1981	Mr Ḥusayn Muṭlaq	Hamadán	Executed (LSA)
57.	22 June 1981	Mr Buzurg ʿAlavíyán	Teheran	Executed
58.	22 June 1981	Mr Háshim Farnúsh	Teheran	Executed (AB)
59.	22 June 1981	Mr Farhang Mavaddat	Teheran	Executed
60.	23 June 1981	Dr Masíḥ Farhangí	Teheran	Executed (CBC)
61.	23 June 1981	Mr Badíʿuʾlláh Faríd	Teheran	Executed
62.	23 June 1981	Mr Yaduʾlláh Pústchí	Teheran	Executed
63.	23 June 1981	Mr Varqá Tibyáníyán (Tibyání)	Teheran	Executed
64.	26 July 1981	Mr Kamáluʾd-Dín Bakhtávar	Káshmar, Khurásán	Executed
65.	26 July 1981	Mr Niʿmatuʾlláh Kátib-púr Shahídí	Káshmar, Khurásán	Executed
66.	29 July 1981	Mr Alláh-Virdí Mítháqí	Tabríz	Executed (LSA)
67.	29 July 1981	Mr Manúchihr Kháḍiʿí	Tabríz	Executed (LSA)
68.	29 July 1981	Mr ʿAbduʾl-ʿAlí Asadyárí	Tabríz	Executed (LSA)
69.	29 July 1981	Mr Ḥusayn Asaduʾlláh-Zádih	Tabríz	Executed (LSA)
70.	29 July 1981	Mr Ismáʿíl Zihtáb	Tabríz	Executed (LSA)
71.	29 July 1981	Dr Parvíz Fírúzí	Tabríz	Executed (LSA)
72.	29 July 1981	Mr Mihdí Báhirí	Tabríz	Executed (LSA)
73.	29 July 1981	Mr Ḥabíbuʾlláh Taḥqíqí	Tabríz	Executed
74.	29 July 1981	Dr Masrúr Dakhílí	Tabríz	Executed (AB)

205

No.	Date	Name	Place	Remarks
75.	5 Aug. 1981	Mr Ḥusayn Rastigár-Námdár	Teheran	Executed
76.	29 Aug. 1981	Mr Ḥabíbu'lláh 'Azízí	Teheran	Executed
77.	11 Sep. 1981	Mr 'Aṭá'u'lláh Rawḥání	Dárún, Iṣfahán	Executed
78.	11 Sep. 1981	Mr Aḥmad Riḍvání	Dárún, Iṣfahán	Executed
79.	11 Sep. 1981	Mr Gushtásb Thábit Rásikh	Dárún, Iṣfahán	Executed
80.	11 Sep. 1981	Mr 'Izzat 'Áṭifí	Dárún, Iṣfahán	Executed
81.	11 Sep. 1981	Mr Bahman 'Áṭifí	Dárún, Iṣfahán	Executed
82.	18 Nov. 1981	Mr Sipihr Arfa'	Teheran	Executed

BAHÁ'ÍS (WHOSE NAMES ARE KNOWN) IMPRISONED IN IRAN
As of 15 December, 1981

No.	Date arrest reported	Name	Place
1.	10 Mar. 1979	Mr Parvíz Yazdání	Teheran
2.	6 Feb. 1980	Mr Nuṣratu'lláh Bahrámí	Teheran
3.	6 Feb. 1980	Mr Ḥusayn 'Ábidíyán-Mihr	Teheran
4.	20 Feb. 1980	Mr Badí'u'lláh Makkáríyán	Gunbad Qábús
5.	3 June 1980	Mr Muḥammad-Riḍá Ḥisámí	Shíráz
6.	5 June 1980	Mrs Qudsíyyih Vaḥdat	Shíráz
7.	9 Aug. 1980	Mr Hidáyatu'lláh Íqání	Ábádih

8.	Mr Shamsu'lláh Dhabíhí	?	Bihshahr
9.	Mr Diyá'i'd-Dín Ahmadí	9 Aug. 1980	Bírjand
10.	Mr 'Alí-Akbar Vakílí	9 Aug. 1980	Bírjand
11.	Mr Haydar Tawdí'í	3 Sept. 1980	Shahmírzád
12.	Mr Haydar-'Alí Saná'í	3 Sept. 1980	Shahmírzád
13.	Mr 'Atá'u'lláh Saná'í	3 Sept. 1980	Shahmírzád
14.	Mr Ridvánu'lláh Saná'í	3 Sept. 1980	Shahmírzád
15.	Mr Farrukh Nádirí	13 May 1981	Shíráz
16.	Mr 'Atá'u'lláh Mitháqí	10 July 1981	Mashhad (AB)
17.	Mr Músá Tálibí	19 July 1981	Farídan, Isfahán
18.	Mr Akbar Ja'farí	19 July 1981	Farídan, Isfahán
19.	Mr Khusraw Murádí	19 July 1981	Farídan, Isfahán
20.	Mr Báqir Ishání	19 July 1981	Afús, Isfahán
21.	Mr Taymúr Íshání	19 July 1981	Afús, Isfahán
22.	Mr Manúchihr Ishráqí	19 July 1981	Sháhinshahr, Isfahán
23.	Mr Shahríyár Ishráqí	19 July 1981	Sháhinshahr, Isfahán
24.	Mr Vafá'í	19 July 1981	Sháhinshahr, Isfahán (LSA)
25.	Mr Bizhán Yazdání	19 July 1981	Kalmán, Isfahán (LSA)
26.	Mr Valíyu'lláh Dánish	19 July 1981	Kalmán, Isfahán (LSA)
27.	Mr Amírí	19 July 1981	Kalmán, Isfahán (LSA)
28.	Mr Kámrán Yazdání	19 July 1981	Kalmán, Isfahán
29.	Mr Husayn Nayyirí	19 July 1981	Isfahán
30.	Mr Bahrám Mudrik	19 July 1981	Isfahán

No.	Date arrest reported	Name	Place
31.	19 July 1981	Mr Luṭfu'lláh Humáyúní	Iṣfahán
32.	19 July 1981	Mr Bahrám Muṭṭahar	Iṣfahán
33.	19 July 1981	Mr Bahrám Sharífí	Iṣfahán
34.	19 July 1981	Mr Humáyúní	Iṣfahán (21 years old)
35.	19 July 1981	Mr Humáyúní	Iṣfahán (teenager)
36.	19 July 1981	Mr Maḥmúd Mitháqí	Teheran (Kúy-i-Síná) (LSA)
37.	19 July 1981	Mr Amru'lláh Ḥusayní	Teheran (Kúy-i-Síná) (LSA)
38.	19 July 1981	Mr Ṭálibí	Karaj (Garm-Darrih)
39.	22 July 1981	Mr Níkjú	Mashhad
40.	28 July 1981	Mr Hidáyatu'lláh Jamshídí	Yazd
41.	28 July 1981	Mr 'Aṭá'u'lláh Tashakkur	Yazd
42.	31 July 1981	Mr 'Alí-Akbar Farrukh	Yazd
43.	31 July 1981	Mr Akhtar-Khávarí	Yazd
44.	9 Aug. 1981	Mr Furúhar	Karaj
45.	9 Aug. 1981	Mrs Furúhar	Karaj
46.	9 Aug. 1981	Mr Ḥaq Paykar	Karaj
47.	11 Aug. 1981	Mr Mihrigání	Yazd
48.	12 Aug. 1981	Mr Jamshíd Pústchí	Shíráz
49.	12 Aug. 1981	Mr Hidáyat Siyávushí	Shíráz
50.	12 Aug. 1981	Mr Farhád Qudrat	Shíráz
51.	23 Aug. 1981	Mr Rajabníyá	Mashhad (LSA)
52.	23 Aug. 1981	Mr 'Abdu'lláhí	Mashhad (LSA)

No.	Name	Date	Location
53.	Mr Íqání	23 Aug. 1981	Bábá-Salmán
54.	Mr Ashjárí	7 Sept. 1981	Ardibíl, Adhirbáyján
55.	Mr Ittihádí	28 Sept. 1981	Yazd
56.	Mrs Gívih Murádiyán	28 Sept. 1981	Yazd
57.	Mr Kárgar	28 Sept. 1981	Yazd
58.	Mrs Tashakkur Khurram	28 Sept. 1981	Yazd
59.	Mr Púr-Khursand	28 Sept. 1981	Yazd
60.	Mr Sha'bán Yúsifiyán	28 Sept. 1981	Teheran
61.	Mrs Munírih Yúsifiyán	28 Sept. 1981	Teheran
62.	Mr Yadu'lláh Lámí	28 Sept. 1981	Teheran
63.	Mrs Mahín Lámí	28 Sept. 1981	Teheran
64.	Mrs Mas'údih 'Azízí	28 Sept. 1981	Teheran
65.	Mr Husayn Vahdat-i-Haq	12 Oct. 1981	Teheran
66.	Mr 'Atá'u'lláh Misbáh	13 Oct. 1981	Rasht
67.	Mr Farzín Misbáh	13 Oct. 1981	Rasht
68.	Mr 'Atá'u'lláh Mushrif-Zádih	13 Oct. 1981	Rasht
69.	Mr Furúghí	13 Oct. 1981	Teheran
70.	Mr Jalál Payraví	22 Oct. 1981	Urúmíyyih (AB)
71.	Mr Qurá'i-Nizhád	26 Oct. 1981	Shíráz (sentenced to 10 years imprisonment)
72.	Mr Ridván Rawháni	26 Oct. 1981	Shíráz
73.	*Mr Kúrush Talá'i	3 Nov. 1981	Teheran (LSA)
74.	*Mr Khusraw Muhandisí	3 Nov. 1981	Teheran (LSA)

* Executed 4 Jan. 1982.

210

No.	Date arrest reported	Name	Place
75.	3 Nov. 1981	*Mr Iskandar ʿAzízí	Teherán (LSA)
76.	3 Nov. 1981	*Mr Fatḥuʾlláh Firdawsí	Teherán (LSA)
77.	3 Nov. 1981	*Mr ʿAṭáʾuʾlláh Yávarí	Teherán (LSA)
78.	3 Nov. 1981	*Mrs S͟hívá Asaduʾlláh-Zádih	Teherán (LSA)
79.	3 Nov. 1981	Mr Manúchihr Baqá	Teherán
80.	3 Nov. 1981	*Mrs S͟hídrukh Baqá	Teherán
81.	6 Dec. 1981	Mr Amínyán	Teherán
82.	7 Dec. 1981	Mr Akbar Háshimí	Rafsanján
83.	7 Dec. 1981	Mr ʿInáyatuʾlláh Sifídvas͟h	Ras͟ht
84.	7 Dec. 1981	Mr Nasír Nabílí	Ras͟ht
85.	14 Dec. 1981	†Mr Kámrán Ṣamímí	Teherán (NSA)
86.	14 Dec. 1981	†Mrs Z͟hínús Maḥmúdí	Teherán (NSA)
87.	14 Dec. 1981	†Mr Maḥmúd Majd͟húb	Teherán (NSA)
88.	14 Dec. 1981	†Mr Jalál ʿAzízí	Teherán (NSA)
89.	14 Dec. 1981	†Mr Mihdí Amín Amín	Teherán (NSA)
90.	14 Dec. 1981	†Mr Sírús Raws͟haní	Teherán (NSA)
91.	14 Dec. 1981	†Mr ʿIzzatuʾlláh Furúhí	Teherán (NSA)
92.	14 Dec. 1981	†Mr Qudratuʾlláh Rawḥání	Teherán (NSA)
93.	14 Dec. 1981	Mr D͟huquʾlláh Muʾmin	Teherán
94.	14 Dec. 1981	Mrs Farídih Ṣamímí	Teherán

* Executed 4 Jan. 1982.
† Executed 27 Dec. 1981.

211

BAHÁ'ÍS MISSING IN IRAN

No.	Date first missed	Name	Place
1.	24 May 1979	Mr Shaykh Muḥammad Muvaḥḥid	Teheran
2.	11 Nov. 1979	Dr 'Alímurád Dávúdí	Teheran (NSA)
3.	3 Jan. 1980	Mr Rúḥí Rawshaní	Teheran (LSA)
4.	21 Aug. 1980	Mr 'Abdu'l-Ḥusayn Taslímí	Teheran (NSA)
5.	21 Aug. 1980	Mr Húshang Maḥmúdí	Teheran (NSA)
6.	21 Aug. 1980	Mr Ibráhím Raḥmání	Teheran (NSA)
7.	21 Aug. 1980	Dr Ḥusayn Nají	Teheran (NSA)
8.	21 Aug. 1980	Mr Manúhir Qá'im-Maqámí	Teheran (NSA)
9.	21 Aug. 1980	Mr 'Aṭá'u'lláh Muqarrabí	Teheran (NSA)
10.	21 Aug. 1980	Mr Yúsif Qadímí	Teheran (NSA)
11.	21 Aug. 1980	Mrs Bahíyyih Nádirí	Teheran (NSA)
12.	21 Aug. 1980	Dr Kámbíz Ṣádiqzádih	Teheran (NSA)
13.	21 Aug. 1980	Dr Yúsif 'Abbásíyán	Teheran (AB)
14.	21 Aug. 1980	Dr Hishmatu'lláh Rawḥání	Teheran (AB)

Stop Press

The following items of information were disseminated throughout the Bahá'í World Community after this book was sent for publication. They clearly reveal the relentless continuance of the bitter persecution of the Bahá'ís in Iran.

November 2, 1981

ENGLISH TEXT CIRCULAR LETTER ISLAMIC MINISTRY FOREIGN AFFAIRS FOLLOWS:

THE ISLAMIC REPUBLIC OF IRAN
MINISTRY OF FOREIGN AFFAIRS

OFFICE: DEPUTY FOR EDUCATIONAL AND CONSULATE AFFAIRS
NO.: 17/533-10/4462
DATE: 21/5/1360 (12 AUGUST 1981)

STRICTLY CONFIDENTIAL-URGENT-DIRECT

IN THE NAME OF HIM WHO IS EXALTED

CIRCULAR LETTER TO ALL REPRESENTATIVES OF THE
ISLAMIC REPUBLIC OF IRAN IN FOREIGN COUNTRIES

FROM THE DATE OF THIS CIRCULAR LETTER, ALL REPRESENTA-TIVES ARE REQUIRED TO CAREFULLY PREPARE THE LIST OF THE NAMES OF ALL BAHA'IS RESIDING WITHIN THEIR JURIS-DICTION, AND THE NAMES OF ANTI-REVOLUTIONARIES, ES-PECIALLY THE SO-CALLED STUDENTS. THESE LISTS SHOULD BE SENT TO US. REPRESENTATIVES SHOULD ALSO REFRAIN FROM EXTENDING THE PASSPORTS OF THESE INDIVIDUALS. ONLY LAISSEZ-PASSER DOCUMENTS MAY BE ISSUED TO THEM.

DEPUTY FOR EDUCATION AND CONSULATE AFFAIRS,
(SIGNED)
  JAVAD MANSURI

November 5, 1981

FOLLOWING GRAVE DEVELOPMENTS REPORTED FROM IRAN:

1. REFERENCE OUR CABLE 26 MAY 1981 WORK ON BUILDING ROAD DESIGNED RUN THROUGH SITE BAB'S HOLY HOUSE SHIRAZ BEING ACTIVELY RESUMED. RECENT REPORT INDICATES WORK STEADILY PROGRESSING APPROACHING SACRED PRECINCTS.
2. OFFICE NATIONAL ASSEMBLY BROKEN INTO PAPERS FILES REMOVED.
3. SIX MEMBERS LOCAL ASSEMBLY TEHERAN SUMMARILY ARRESTED WHILE IN SESSION. COUPLE IN WHOSE HOME MEETING WAS HELD HAVE ALSO BEEN DETAINED.
4. GOVERNMENT IRAN HAS RECENTLY INSTRUCTED ITS CONSULAR REPRESENTATIVES EVERYWHERE COMPILE LIST BAHA'IS RESIDING AREAS THEIR RESPONSIBILITY AND HENCEFORTH REFRAIN FROM EXTENDING PASSPORTS IRANIAN BAHA'IS.

November 5, 1981

NON-BAHA'I EYEWITNESS FRIENDLY TO BAHA'IS JUST RELEASED FROM PRISON HAS REPORTED HAVING SEEN PRISON GUARDS SAVAGELY BEATING TORTURING KURUSH TALA'I, ISKANDAR AZIZI, AND FATHU'LLAH FIRDAWSI COURSE INTERROGATIONS IN ORDER EXTORT FROM THEM ANSWERS REGARDING FINANCIAL DEALINGS AND TRANSFERS OVERSEAS.

December 10, 1981

DISTRESSED REPORT RECENT DEVELOPMENTS IRAN EVIDENCE FURTHER PERSECUTIONS ATROCITIES AGAINST DEFENSELESS BELIEVERS CRADLE FAITH:

1. HOUSE OF BAHAULLAH IN TAKUR, PREVIOUSLY CONFISCATED, HAS NOW BEEN TOTALLY DEMOLISHED AND THIS BAHA'I HOLY PLACE INCLUDING LAND AND GARDENS OFFERED FOR SALE TO PUBLIC BY AUTHORITIES.

2. BAHA'I CEMETERY TEHERAN SEIZED ON SATURDAY 5 DE-
CEMBER BY ORDER REVOLUTIONARY COURT, 5 CARE-
TAKERS AND 8 TEMPORARY WORKERS ARRESTED, AND
CEMETERY CLOSED. BAHA'IS FEARFUL DESECRATION
GRAVES. TENS OF THOUSANDS BAHA'IS TEHERAN NOW
WITHOUT BURIAL GROUND. THIS RECENT INDECENT ACT
STILL ANOTHER EXAMPLE EVIL DESIGNS ELIMINATE BAHA'I
COMMUNITY THAT COUNTRY.

3. IN RUSTAQ, VILLAGE NEAR YAZD, DURING SECOND HALF
NOVEMBER 8 BAHA'IS, INCLUDING 2 WOMEN, ARRESTED. 20
BAHA'I HOMES SEALED, 5 EMPTIED OF FURNITURE.

4. NO BAHA'IS HAVE BEEN INCLUDED IN RECENTLY PUBLI-
CIZED AMNESTY. IN FACT, NEW ARRESTS HAVE BEEN MADE
AND BAHA'IS ARE STILL HELD IN PRISONS IN TEHERAN,
YAZD, URUMIYYIH, BIRJAND, MASHHAD, KARAJ AND
ISFAHAN.

5. AN ISLAMIC SOCIETY OSTENSIBLY FORMED 'TO FIGHT
AGAINST RELIGIOUS TRANSGRESSIONS' HAS TAKEN LIB-
ERTY TO RAID AND SEAL BAHA'I HOMES IN TEHERAN AND
TO CONFISCATE PROPERTIES. GROUP HAS ITS OWN PRISONS.
AT LEAST 4 BAHA'IS BELIEVED TAKEN BY THIS GROUP AND
PLACED IN ITS PRISONS.

December 14, 1981

HAVE JUST RECEIVED DISTRESSING REPORT EIGHT MEMBERS
NATIONAL ASSEMBLY IRAN WHILE IN SESSION ARRESTED
TOGETHER WITH TWO OTHER BELIEVERS IN HOME WHERE
MEETING WAS HELD. TWO WOMEN AMONG TEN DETAINEES.
AUTHORITY RESPONSIBLE FOR ARRESTS AND LOCATION
PRISON STILL UNIDENTIFIED. INFORM YOUR GOVERNMENTS
AND MEDIA.

December 29, 1981

WITH HEAVY HEARTS INFORM FRIENDS THROUGHOUT WORLD
EIGHT MEMBERS NATIONAL ASSEMBLY IRAN ARRESTED 13
DECEMBER WERE EXECUTED 27 DECEMBER. THEY ARE:

MR KAMRAN SAMIMI
MRS ZHINUS MAHMUDI
MR MAHMUD MAJDHUB
MR JALAL AZIZI
MR MIHDI AMIN AMIN
MR SIRUS RAWSHANI
MR IZZATULLAH FURUHI
MR QUDRATULLAH RAWHANI

FAMILIES NOT NOTIFIED OF ARRESTS, TRIAL, EXECUTIONS. BODIES BURIED UNCEREMONIOUSLY IN BARREN FIELD RESERVED BY GOVERNMENT FOR INFIDELS. INFORMATION DISCOVERED FORTUITOUSLY. GOVERNMENT AUTHORITIES TOTALLY SILENT, UNCOOPERATIVE.

THIS HEINOUS ACT CAUSES US FEAR THAT MEMBERS PREVIOUS NATIONAL ASSEMBLY AND TWO AUXILIARY BOARD MEMBERS WHO DISAPPEARED AUGUST 1980, AS WELL AS TWO OTHERS WHOSE WHEREABOUTS UNKNOWN OVER TWO YEARS, HAVE SUFFERED SAME FATE. NAMES THESE HEROIC DEDICATED SERVANTS BLESSED BEAUTY ARE:

AUXILIARY BOARD MEMBERS
DR YUSIF ABBASIYAN
DR HISHMATULLAH RAWHANI

NATIONAL ASSEMBLY MEMBERS
DR ALIMURAD DAVUDI
MR ABDUL-HUSAYN TASLIMI
MR HUSHANG MAHMUDI
MR IBRAHIM RAHMANI
DR HUSAYN NAJI
MR MANUHIR QAIM-MAQAMI
MR ATAULLAH MUQARRABI
MR YUSIF QADIMI
MRS BAHIYYIH NADIRI
DR KAMBIZ SADIQZADIH

MEMBER LOCAL ASSEMBLY TEHERAN
MR RUHI RAWSHANI

PROMINENT TEACHER
MR MUHAMMAD MUVAHHID

January 5, 1982

PRESIDENT SUPREME COURT AYATOLLAH ARDIBILI IS RE-
PORTED BY NEWS SERVICES TO HAVE DENIED EXECUTION
EIGHT MEMBERS NATIONAL ASSEMBLY IRAN. YOU SHOULD
CATEGORICALLY CONFIRM TO MEDIA OUR PREVIOUS INFOR-
MATION REGARDING EXECUTIONS CORRECT. WE CONVINCED
EXECUTIONS WERE PLANNED TO BE KEPT SECRET BUT WERE
DISCOVERED FORTUITOUSLY. BAHA'I INTERNATIONAL COM-
MUNITY REQUESTING SECRETARY GENERAL UNITED NATIONS
INVESTIGATE. URGE YOU APPEAL YOUR GOVERNMENT LEND
SUPPORT BAHA'I INTERNATIONAL COMMUNITY REQUEST.

January 7, 1982

BAHA'I INTERNATIONAL COMMUNITY CABLING FOLLOWING
TEXT TO AYATOLLAH KHOMEINI, PRIME MINISTER MIR HUSAYN
MUSAVI, AND PRESIDENT SUPREME COURT AYATOLLAH
MUSAVI ARDIBILI:

NEWS RECENT SECRET EXECUTION EIGHT MEMBERS NATIONAL
ASSEMBLY BAHA'IS IRAN, AND SEVEN OTHERS, SIX OF WHOM
WERE MEMBERS LOCAL ASSEMBLY TEHERAN, HAS SHOCKED
BAHA'IS ENTIRE WORLD. TOTAL NUMBER BAHA'IS WHOSE
MARTYRDOMS OFFICIALLY ACKNOWLEDGED HAS NOW
REACHED NINETY-SEVEN. FOURTEEN OTHERS, KNOWN TO
HAVE DISAPPEARED, FEARED TO HAVE SUFFERED SAME FATE.
HUNDREDS IMPRISONED THROUGHOUT COUNTRY ON
CHARGES WITHOUT SUBSTANTIATING EVIDENCE. WE CATE-
GORICALLY DENY TRUTH THESE ACCUSATIONS.
AS BAHA'IS IRAN ARE RIGIDLY DENIED OPPORTUNITY PUB-
LICLY PRESENT THEIR CASE, DEFEND THEIR RIGHTS, PROVE
THEIR INNOCENCE, AND ALL DOORS APPEAL THEIR CASE
CLOSED BEFORE THEM, WE THEREFORE APPEAL TO YOU ON

THEIR BEHALF IN NAME OF BAHA'I COMMUNITIES IN 164
INDEPENDENT COUNTRIES OF THE WORLD:

1. TO ISSUE IMMEDIATE INSTRUCTIONS STOP SUMMARY
   ARRESTS EXECUTIONS,
2. TO REQUIRE THOSE RESPONSIBLE PRODUCE PUBLISH DOCU-
   MENTS WHICH HAVE FORMED BASIS CONVICTION BAHA'IS AS
   SO-CALLED SPIES,
3. TO EXTEND TO BAHA'IS AS LAW-ABIDING CITIZENS, AND AS
   A COMMUNITY, INALIENABLE RIGHT TO PUBLICLY DEFEND
   THEMSELVES DISPROVE MALICIOUS ACCUSATIONS FALSE
   CHARGES.

WE LAY BEFORE YOU FATE THESE LOYAL CITIZENS ABOUT
WHOSE INNOCENCE, TRUE LOVE FOR IRAN AND REVERENCE
FOR SPIRIT ISLAM YOU SHOULD HAVE NO DOUBT. WE PRAY THE
ALMIGHTY MAY GUIDE YOU THIS ELEVENTH HOUR TO DIS-
CHARGE SACRED INESCAPABLE RESPONSIBILITIES BEFORE GOD
AND MAN.

BAHA'I INTERNATIONAL COMMUNITY

January 7, 1982

INFORMATION JUST RECEIVED SIX MEMBERS LOCAL SPIRITUAL
ASSEMBLY TEHERAN TOGETHER WITH WOMAN BELIEVER IN
WHOSE HOME ARRESTS WERE MADE ON SECOND NOVEMBER
WERE SECRETLY EXECUTED ON FOURTH JANUARY. INFOR-
MATION OBTAINED FORTUITOUSLY BY RELATIVES FRIENDS
MARTYRS. NAMES THESE VALIANT SOULS ARE:

MR KURUSH TALAI
MR KHUSRAW MUHANDISI
MR ISKANDAR AZIZI
MR FATHULLAH FIRDAWSI
MR ATAULLAH YAVARI
MRS SHIVA MAHMUDI ASADULLAH-ZADIH
HOSTESS: MRS SHIDRUKH AMIR-KIYA BAQA

Instruction given by the headmaster of "Ráhnamá' i Kúy-i-Maskan va Shahrsází", dated 13.7.1360 (5 October 1981)

Emblem of the Islamic Republic of Iran
Ministry of Education, Department of Education, Province of Yazd

This is to certify that Nádir Báqirí Qalát Pá'in, son of Muhammad, I.D. card No. 226-1346, who has been a student of this school in the academic year of 1360/61 (1981/82) and who has been studying until 13.7.1360 (5 October 1981), is now forbidden to study in this school because of his being a Bahá'í. This decision is in accordance with the circular letter dated 12.7.1360 (4 October 1981), No. 28664, issued by the Education office of the province of Yazd.

(signed),
Headmaster of the school, Ahmad Zamání

Facsimile of the original Persian (with English translation) of a typical expulsion order dismissing a Bahá'í child from school as a result of his refusal to recant his Faith. The order indicates the fate of thousands of Bahá'í children.

February 4, 1982 (Press Release from Strasbourg)

Parliamentary Assembly of Council of Europe Adopts Resolution Calling on Iran to Grant Freedom of Religion to Baha'is

A TWO-HOUR DEBATE ON PERSECUTIONS IN IRAN TOOK PLACE ON FRIDAY, 29 JANUARY 1982, IN THE PARLIAMENTARY ASSEMBLY OF THE COUNCIL OF EUROPE. THE DEBATE CULMINATED IN THE UNANIMOUS ADOPTION OF A RESOLUTION CALLING UPON THE GOVERNMENT OF IRAN TO EXTEND CONSTITUTIONAL GUARANTEES TO THE BAHA'I COMMUNITY OF THAT COUNTRY. THE RESOLUTION ALSO CALLED ON THE GOVERNMENTS OF THE TWENTY-ONE MEMBER STATES OF THE COUNCIL OF EUROPE TO USE EVERY OPPORTUNITY, INCLUDING EUROPEAN COMMUNITY AND UNITED NATIONS CHANNELS, TO CONVINCE THE IRANIAN GOVERNMENT OF THE NECESSITY TO RESPECT INTERNATIONAL CONVENTIONS TO WHICH IT IS A PARTY.

IN SUMMING UP THE DEBATE, THE CHAIRMAN OF THE POLITICAL AFFAIRS COMMITTEE CONGRATULATED THE RAPPORTEUR ON HIS FINE REPORT AND SAID THAT THE NUMBER OF SPEAKERS, IN A DEBATE WHICH HAD BEEN ESSENTIALLY NON-POLITICAL (IT HAD DEALT PRIMARILY WITH RELIGIOUS PERSECUTION), WAS EXTREMELY UNUSUAL AND TESTIFIED TO THE HORROR AND REVULSION FELT BY THE ASSEMBLY AT THE MASSIVE PERSECUTION OF THE BAHA'IS IN IRAN.